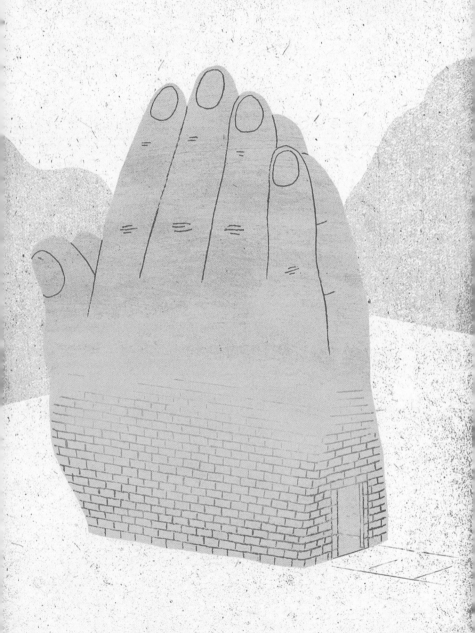

Praise for

The Happiness Prayer

"One of our truly thoughtful and charismatic young leaders, Evan Moffic provides in captivating prose the wisdom and comfort of Jewish teachings for Jews and Gentile alike."

—David Ellenson, chancellor, Hebrew
Union College-Jewish Institute of Religion

"The true goal of religion, of union with the Almighty, is not order, or a legalistic life, or even worldly success, but something more elusive, and more valuable: joy. In his delightful new book, Rabbi Moffic reveals the hidden elements of Jewish wisdom and prayer that can lead us to a happy life. 'Blessed are those who are happy!' might be Rabbi Moffic's entirely ancient and beautifully new beatitude."

—James Martin, SJ, author of *Jesus: A Pilgrimage*

"The longer I live, and the more I'm faced with the inescapable reality of pain in life, the more I search for and surround myself with people who exude joy. Men and women who know how to dance in the rain. My friend, Rabbi Evan Moffic, is a shining example. It's impossible to be in a bad mood when I'm with him. And this book delivers that joyful spirit directly to you."

—Michele Cushatt, author of *I Am: A 60-Day
Journey to Knowing Who You Are Because of Who He Is*

"Rabbi Moffic has written a beautiful book about what Jewish wisdom can teach us all about how to lead a more meaningful life. Full of moving stories and wise advice, THE HAPPINESS PRAYER shows that true happiness lies in serving others and cultivating our best selves. This is a book that encourages reflection and offers hope."

—Emily Esfahani Smith, TED speaker
and author of *The Power of Meaning*

"Want to know where to put your energy for a life that has maximal meaning, connection, and opportunities to grow as a person? Read THE HAPPINESS PRAYER. Rabbi Evan Moffic masterfully takes us on a powerful journey through the wisdom of our tradition and the complexities of the human heart. This happiness isn't about quick fixes and instant gratification—rather, it's the recipe for something much more long-lasting and sustaining."

—Rabbi Danya Ruttenberg, author of *Nurture the Wow: Finding Spirituality in the Frustration, Boredom, Tears, Poop, Desperation, Wonder, and Radical Amazement of Parenting*

"With sensitivity and insight, Rabbi Evan Moffic offers ancient wisdom to give us meaning and mooring amidst the challenges of our daily lives."

—Rabbi David Stern, president, Central Conference of American Rabbis

"A much needed reminder—in a culture of seeking—that happiness can be a return to something ancient; Evan Moffic's insights and humanity fill the pages of THE HAPPINESS PRAYER, shining beauty and affirmation on the wisdom of a two-thousand-year-old prayer, and making it accessible to anyone yearning for a more meaningful life."

—Dan Ain, founder of Because Jewish and former rabbi in residence at 92Y

"Rabbi Moffic captures a primary contemporary pursuit—happiness—and refracts it through anecdotes, rabbinic wisdom, and popular culture to remind us that that the path to happiness is right before us at all times. Its wisdom is like the prize inside of a box of crackerjacks—a simple pleasure."

—Rabbi Lori Shapiro, The Open Temple

The Happiness Prayer

The Happiness Prayer

Ancient Jewish Wisdom
for the Best Way *to* Live Today

RABBI EVAN MOFFIC

CENTER
STREET

New York Nashville

Center Street
Hachette Book Group
1290 Avenue of the Americas, New York, NY 10104
centerstreet.com
twitter.com/centerstreet

First Edition: September 2017

Center Street is a division of Hachette Book Group, Inc. The Center Street name and logo are trademarks of Hachette Book Group, Inc.

The publisher is not responsible for websites (or their content) that are not owned by the publisher.

The Hachette Speakers Bureau provides a wide range of authors for speaking events. To find out more, go to www.HachetteSpeakersBureau.com or call (866) 376-6591.

Library of Congress Cataloging-in-Publication Data

Names: Moffic, Evan, 1978– author.
Title: The happiness prayer : ancient Jewish wisdom for the best way to live today / Rabbi Evan Moffic.
Description: First edition. | New York ; Nashville : Center Street, [2017]
Identifiers: LCCN 2017016321| ISBN 9781478918066 (hardback) | ISBN 9781478918080 (ebook)
Subjects: LCSH: Judaism—Essence, genius, nature. | Happiness—Religious aspects—Judaism. | Jewish way of life. | Mishnah. Peah—Meditations. | Moffic, Evan, 1978– | BISAC: RELIGION / Judaism / General. | SELF-HELP / Personal Growth / Happiness. | RELIGION / Judaism / Reform. | RELIGION / Judaism / Conservative.
Classification: LCC BM565 .M583 2017 | DDC 296—dc23
LC record available at https://lccn.loc.gov/2017016321

ISBNs: 978-1-4789-1806-6 (hardcover), 978-1-4789-1808-0 (ebook)

Printed in the United States of America

LSC-C

10 9 8 7 6 5 4 3 2 1

To Congregation Solel for trusting me to be your rabbi, and for giving me the opportunity to lead, write, speak, and grow.

"I have learned much from my teachers, more from my colleagues, and the most from my students."
(The Talmud, Tractate Ta'anit, 7a)

Contents

The Happiness Prayer

The Smiling Rabbi

A few years ago my friend started a ritual in her home. When she got home from work, she would ask her two kids the following: "On a scale of one to ten, how would you rate your day?" The first time she did it, the oldest daughter thought for a while. Then she answered, "6.125." She recounted what her teachers and friends had said to her, what she'd learned, whom she'd sat with at lunch, and how she had been late for dance practice. Delivering the answer took about five minutes.

The second daughter responded with a question. "What is the highest, Mom?" "Ten." "Well," she said with a smile, "it was a ten!" Then she skipped out of the room.

Some of us seem wired for happiness. We make smiley faces on our papers. We see a glass half-full. We answer the phone with a cheerful hello. Others of us are more like the older daughter. We evaluate every conversation. We always imagine what might go wrong in an upcoming meeting. We look up at the sky and see the clouds.

Which one are you? Do you tend to look for the good? Or do you worry about what might go wrong? This book will give you a clearer picture of yourself. It will also give you a path for uncovering a deeper happiness—a sense of meaning and purpose in your life. It will do so by exposing you to the words of a special Hebrew prayer called Eilu Devarim (pronounced ay-lu dehvar-eem). The name means "These are the words." It was written two thousand years ago and consists of ten short verses. It has been a part of Jewish worship for several hundred years, and I have been saying it every morning for most of my life.

I discovered its real power, though, during a painful time. I had gone through most of life with the attitude of my friend's younger daughter. I had loving parents. I'd studied at my dream college. I'd found my ideal calling as a rabbi. Most days had been tens. My wife had said my constant smiles were the thing that most attracted her. Sure, there had been setbacks, but even those had seemed to lead ultimately to something better.

Then age thirty brought the opportunity of a lifetime. I became the lead rabbi of a large and historic congregation. I felt lucky and blessed, and I knew I could help the community do amazing things. But the initial excitement quickly turned into a recognition of the reality of my new situation. Two thousand people turned to me for help with the pains and tragedies of life—broken marriages, problems with their children, the deaths of parents and grandparents, and much more. In my earlier positions, I'd always had a backup. Now I was supposed to have all the answers. Did I really have what it took? Did I have enough experience and empathy to help with life-and-death choices? Judaism rarely offers easy answers to hard questions. It is a faith that values debate and struggle over dogma and certainty. I wondered whether I could really guide the congregation looking to me for wisdom and truth.

I also lost a close friend—a medical resident with everything going for him—to suicide. My wife and I had just had a baby, and it had not been an easy pregnancy. Our oldest child had medical problems. Nothing was the way it was supposed to be. The happy rabbi—the one whose parents had given him a "What, Me Worry?" sign for his office—questioned his calling and his faith.

Through these painful times, the words of the Eilu Devarim prayer took on new meaning. I realized the words I was saying were not directed only toward God; I was also saying them to myself. And the prayer saved me. It gave me a new perspective. It infused vitality into my leadership and family. It renewed in me the joy of learning and teaching and serving as a moral and spiritual guide. People now call me "the smiling rabbi."

The prayer did not always reveal easy answers. But it became a compass pointing me back in the right direction. It can do the same for you. It works whether you are Jewish or not, religious or not. It works not because you get some magical feeling after saying it. It works because of the truths and practices it reveals. It works because you bring its teachings into your life. It is not a typical prayer in that you just say it. It is an active prayer because you live it. The magic is not in the words. It is in the way you use the words to change yourself.

The prayer also works because it illuminates a new approach toward happiness. The modern English word *happiness* comes from the Middle English *hap*, as in *happenstance* and *haphazard*. The origin suggests that a happy life is a result of randomness and luck. The Hebrew word for happiness—*simcha*—demands intention. It comes from an intentional pursuit of joy amid community. That difference suggests that finding happiness is a choice. It is a choice available to all of us. Happiness is not a destination. It is the path itself. That's what we find revealed in the Eilu Devarim prayer, along with much else. The prayer doesn't only get us through hard times. Its lessons sustain us through life.

Perhaps you have lost a loved one, gone through a divorce, or lost a job. Perhaps you are struggling to forgive someone who hurt you. Perhaps you feel you are missing your sense of purpose, and life seems to be passing you by. Perhaps you are just overwhelmed with all that life throws at you. You may be asking yourself if you will ever find happiness. I have been there—as a person, and as a rabbi in the trenches of life with my congregation. And I have discovered that everyone can find happiness because happiness is not a thing. It is a way of life. Each of us can discover meaning in our struggles, our choices, and our achievements. Each of us can sustain that meaning through ongoing practices. This discovery is not instant. But it is within our reach. This prayer clears the way for us. It gets us back on the road to happiness.

The Structure

The prayer begins with a statement of its purpose. It uses a financial metaphor. Our actions represent an investment of our time. The interest on this investment is our happiness. Like financial interest, it compounds. In other words, the longer we follow these lessons, the more our happiness grows.

Here is my paraphrase of the Hebrew original of the prayer.

How will you find happiness in this world and peace in the world to come? By learning these wisdom practices from your ancestors:

Honor those who gave you life
Be kind
Keep learning
Invite others into your life
Be there when others need you
Celebrate good times

Support yourself and others during times of loss
Pray with intention
Forgive
Look inside and commit

You are the hero of this book because you can take action today. You can listen for and act on the truths captured in this prayer, even just one of them. Each chapter will reveal ways I have learned and acted on these truths, and ways in which they have changed the lives of those I teach and lead. These stories will not only guide you in living these truths. You will also get a clear and inspiring understanding of *why* they work. We are human beings, not robots. Knowing our *why* will keep us more committed and engaged. There will be times when we fail. There will be times when we lose confidence. Knowing the *why* keeps us going. In other words, the more you understand where these wisdom practices come from and the ways in which they guide our lives, the happier you can be.

Each chapter will also give you an inside look at the writings of the Jewish sages who formulated this wisdom tradition and sustained it over thousands of years. Many of their insights have also found expression in psychology, social work, spirituality, counseling, and much more, but you will grasp the core insights into human nature that began it all. You are about to begin a journey that will change the way you look at your life.

Real Happiness Matters Now More than Ever

It's time to focus on this journey to real happiness because so much distracts us from getting there. A recent study found that every day we encounter more than three thousand commercials.

They come on TV, on billboards, on the radio, on YouTube videos. And they all have the same message. Something is making you unhappy. You deserve to be happy. We have a product to make you happy. Buy it from us now.

The only problem is that all our possessions and all our purchasing fail to make us happy. We have more stuff today than ever. But we are not any happier. We are more anxious and on edge. We are more uncertain about the future. We feel more distant from the values and practices that once gave clarity to life. A 2016 survey conducted by the Harris Poll found that only one in three Americans reports feeling very happy with their life, and Generation Y (those born between 1980 and 2000) are the "most stressed generation."

We know life should not be this way. But we cope with it by escaping to food, to addictions, or to unhealthy relationships. We blame others. Or we just give up. We put up with jobs that make us miserable. We decide life is unfair.

The Eilu Devarim prayer reminds us there is another way. I call it a prayer because we recite and sing it during a worship service, but it is really a list of truths. These truths, as we will see, came out of the struggle of the Jewish community. The rabbis who wrote them down two thousand years ago faced centuries of persecution from the Roman Empire. The Jews were a beleaguered people who had to teach their wisdom in secret. They knew that the survival of their way of life depended on their ability to pass it on to their children. They needed to build strong communities and help each other cope with and thrive in an anxious and ever-changing world.

Their challenges are also our challenges. Yes, we enjoy many more things and greater political freedom than they did, but we still yearn to find meaning and purpose in a rapidly changing world. We still seek real happiness in a world filled with distraction and frustration. Our technologies have changed. Our dreams have not. That's why Eilu Devarim offers great wisdom. That's why it can transform your life.

You have before you not only a happiness prayer, but a checklist for a meaningful life. It has been tested over the last two thousand years. If you can do what it says, you will be happier—perhaps happier than you have ever thought possible.

What the Chicago Cubs Taught Me about Happiness

"All of life is a challenge of not being distracted from the greatness that we are."

—Rabbi Yitzhak Kirzner

I'm a Chicagoan. While my dad grew up on the city's South Side and roots for the Chicago White Sox, I lead a congregation on the city's North Side and root for the Chicago Cubs. The White Sox won the World Series in 2005. When I started serving my current congregation, the Cubs had not won a world series since 1908.

Something big happened in 2011. The team's leaders recognized it needed a change. They hired a president of baseball operations by the name of Theo Epstein. In 2004, Epstein had led the Boston Red Sox to their first championship in eighty-six years. He had done so by embracing a certain philosophy of management.

The philosophy focuses on improving the fundamentals that many overlook. It involves focusing on on-base percentage rather than batting average, taking pitchers out of a game after they have thrown a set number of pitches, and recruiting players based on slugging percentage rather than number of home runs. Epstein focused consistently on these fundamentals, whether or not they seemed right for a particular game or season.

During the first few years after he was hired, the Cubs did not improve. Our record remained among the worst in the league. Fans remained despondent. Some wanted to give up on this new plan. Epstein and his defenders responded, in essence, that they were not focused on winning. They were focused on doing the concrete things he had promised. Winning would be a by-product of doing those little things right.

Well, in 2015 things started to change. We had an excellent record. We made it to the division championship. In 2016, just as I was completing this book, we won the World Series for the first time in 108 years! What Epstein had said throughout the first few years now seems prophetic. Winning does not come from hiring the biggest superstar hitter. It doesn't come from drafting the hottest pitcher in the league. It comes from doing certain things faithfully and consistently.

This insight applies not only to baseball. It rings true in our most important pursuit: the pursuit of a happy, satisfying, and meaningful life. Happiness is not something you can get by buying a fast, expensive car. It doesn't come, as I learned, from getting the job you always dreamed of. It does not even come from health or wealth. It comes, like winning in baseball, from doing certain things faithfully and consistently. These practices sustain us through the inevitable pains and downturns of life. What they are—and how each of us can do them—is what we are about to discover.

How to Start

We're not the first generation to seek happiness. The quest for happiness is actually as old as Western civilization. The Greek philosopher Socrates defined the point of life as finding happiness. The last two decades, however, have seen researchers make extraordinary strides in understanding what exact practices make for a happier life. Those practices range from cultivating meaningful relationships to living in the right kind of community (like Denmark, the happiest nation on earth) to daily journaling. All of these activities have merit. But before we analyze them, we have to answer the first challenge. How do we get in the right mind-set? How do we commit ourselves to doing the right things? See, we often know the right thing to do. But how do we get ourselves to do it?

Well, like the Chicago Cubs, we need an adjustment. Even though our problem—how to make choices that make us happier—has been around for centuries, we need a new approach to addressing it. We can't simply try the latest workout system or the newest form of meditation. We can't simply travel to the hottest new destination or read the most recent life-changing book. We need an approach rooted in ancient wisdom.

Put simply, we need faith. At its core, faith is the belief that life has meaning. It is the confidence that we are here on this earth for a reason. Faith is not about grand theological ideas. It is about the everyday choices we make. It is about becoming a person whose life makes a real, positive difference to the people around them. I learned this lesson from my parents and grandparents. But I also saw it in my spiritual home—the synagogue. When I was growing up, my mom brought me to synagogue every Friday night. She sang in the choir. I usually sat and played games.

But one Friday evening I started talking to an older man. His name was Dave Miller. He was a widower. Before retiring he had owned a costume showroom that outfitted the actors at almost all the local theaters. He had an infectious smile. He constantly cracked jokes, most of which were about the length of the rabbi's sermons. We had a game where he would nudge me every time he thought the sermon should conclude. Once he nudged me eighteen times and took a short nap in the middle of that same sermon!

Dave was not rich. He did not have a large family. Yet he was the happiest person I ever met. I asked him what made him so happy. How did he sustain his optimism and joy? He told me a story.

His wife, Effie, had been diagnosed with rheumatic fever in her late twenties. The diagnosis came shortly before the vaccine for the fever was released. It was a gradually debilitating illness. Doctors told her she would likely die in her early fifties. She lived, however, into her late sixties.

The diagnosis brought Dave's life into perspective. He made each day with his wife and daughter count because he did not know how many days they would have together. They made the synagogue their second home. He went every Friday night with Effie to worship. They made friends during the fellowship hour. They sang and got inspired during prayer. They learned in enrichment classes.

When Effie entered the hospital for the last time, *she was never alone.* Members of the synagogue constantly came to visit. They brought over meals for Dave. One friend even came and blew the shofar (ram's horn) for the Jewish New Year. When she died, the community filled the sanctuary for her funeral service. They told Dave what she'd meant to them. They told him how lucky they felt to have been able to be there with the two of them through her illness and death.

Dave told me that he would not be alive had it not been for this community. They were people he could count on. And he wanted to be that kind of person. Since he knew the fragility of life, he determined to continue to live each day to the fullest. Effie's death, for him, was about much more than burying and losing her. It was, he told me, an affirmation of life—an affirmation that a life well lived is the greatest gift God offers us.

Dave died during my second year of rabbinical school. I delivered a eulogy at his funeral, and doing so reminded me of why I was becoming a rabbi. I was learning so much about Jewish legal codes, biblical grammar, and the finer points of theology. But what really mattered, I said to myself as I wrote the eulogy, was the way faith enhances our lives. In other words, *faith is not only about what we believe, but also about how we live.* Dave was an example of the deep link between faith and happiness.

I ended the eulogy with a quote from Jonathan Sacks, then the chief rabbi of Great Britain. It encapsulates the depth of that link. "Happiness," he said, "is the ability to look back on a life and say: I lived for certain values. I acted on them and was willing to make sacrifices for them. I was part of a family, embracing it and being embraced by it in return. I was a good neighbor, ready to help when needed. I was part of a community, honoring its traditions, participating in its life, sharing its obligations. It is these things that make up happiness in this uncertain world." At its best, faith invites each of us to such a life.

Why Faith Has Worked for Five Thousand Years

I didn't learn of this connection between faith and happiness in seminary. But the evidence for it is not just anecdotal. Research shows that faith is often a critical component of a meaningful and happy life. As Barbara Fredrickson, a leading social psychology scholar, puts it, "Religious practices help people find positive meaning in life, which elicits positive emotions, which in turn broadens the mind and increases personal resources, leading to improved health and well-being." In other words, practices motivated by faith work. Faith is commitment to these practices and the repetition of them. This commitment plus repetition helps us develop the critical character traits and emotional experiences that make for a healthier and happier life. Happiness is a by-product of faith. Before we figure out what this means for us, we need to make an important clarification. *Faith and religion are not the same thing.* Religion is the organized expression and framework for acting upon our faith. Faith is universal, whereas religion is particular. Faith is like love. Religion is the relationship through which we express that love. Faith is poetry. Religion is prose. Faith is the encounter with God. Religion is the behavior through which we embrace the lessons from that encounter. Faith centers on the individual. Religion focuses on the group. You can have faith without being religious. It is more difficult to be religious without faith. The two are linked, but they are not the same.

When it comes to the pursuit of happiness, we learn from them both. Faith is the universal feeling of connection to something larger. Finding ways to cultivate that feeling is essential to the pursuit of happiness. But faith alone is also incomplete. We need the specific practices and behaviors taught within religious systems. I am a rabbi; my religion is Judaism and the practices I follow flow from the texts and traditions held sacred by the Jewish people. This book flows from wisdom I find within a prayer central to Jewish tradition. *But the behaviors it teaches are available to all. No one religion is the sole path to happiness.* That's because of what underlies each religion's particular behaviors: commitment.

Much of the power of religion comes in its focus on *commitment*. We follow certain practices because we have *committed* ourselves to doing so. We do not give to charity, show up for worship, or fast on certain days just because they are nice things to do. We do them because we have voluntarily chosen to live by a set of commitments. It is like getting married. In Western society we generally choose whether we get married and to whom. But once we enter into that marriage, we are bound by commitments that flow from it. If we had no feeling of commitment, there would be little trust or security in the relationship. We would be valuing short-term pleasure over long-term satisfaction. That's why we choose commitments. They lead to a more lasting sense of comfort and well-being.

Changing Our Mind-Set

Happiness is a by-product of living by our commitments to our faith. We do not often think of faith, though, in this way. We tend to think committing to faith gets us a ticket into heaven. We tend to think of it as being about making God happy. *But these commitments aren't only about making God happy. They ultimately make us happy. They reveal the path to true meaning and satisfaction in life.* Long ago faith hewed a path for us, one that has been well trod over thousands of years. And in walking down that path, we have a time-tested guide in our prayer.

And we also have a contemporary guide in the academic discipline of positive psychology. I discovered this school of thought when trying to figure out better ways to guide my congregation. The struggles they faced were often not the ones depicted in the Bible and the texts I'd studied in seminary. Yes, the Bible has wisdom about marriage and death and difficulties with parents and children. But the Bible came into being in a different world. In the past, many accepted its absolute truth.

We do not live in such a world. We seek the proof of science and experience. Thus the discipline of positive psychology—also known as the science of happiness—became an important source for me and my congregation in understanding our prayer. But it did something more than that. It gave me a better appreciation of the true power of faith. It revealed to me the mind-set we need to let the prayer work its magic. The mind-set is a trust in the power of ancient traditions and practices. It is a commitment to the wisdom of the past for the sake of the future.

On a practical level, the faith mind-set pushes us to do some things that may not feel great in the short term, but that enhance our lives in the long term. *It is like a built-in Theo Epstein to help guide our choices and actions.* These are the choices that we can look back on a year later and feel happy to have made. To take a simple example: I fast every year on Yom Kippur, the Jewish Day of Atonement. To do so is a commandment found in the Bible and has been a Jewish tradition for more than four thousand years. Since I am working all day—delivering sermons and leading my congregation in eight hours of prayer—fasting is the last thing I want to do. Yet it enhances my experience of the day and my connection to others. It does not feel right at the moment. But I look back and know I experienced the power of the day.

This is the kind of commitment faith has always nurtured, and ignoring the role of faith in the search for happiness is like going to search for a treasure and throwing away an old map leading directly to it. Faith brings happiness.

Don't take my word for it. Look at the studies of people who have found an authentic life of faith. They live, on average, seven years longer than others. They have more friends. They give more to charity. They are healthier. All of this has been shown by a new science—the study of positive psychology—that gives proof for some of the truths and practices faith teaches.

The Science of Happiness

Positive psychology did not start out to prove the wisdom of our faith traditions. Rather, it began in the early 1990s, when a psychology professor named Martin Seligman started writing about and researching the practices and habits of happy people. He ultimately developed a model whereby our answers to particular questions can help us see where we are succeeding and not succeeding in the pursuit of happiness. The five categories in the model are positive emotion, engagement, relationships, meaning, and accomplishment (PERMA). Our prayer, as we will see, leads to all of them.

Positive emotion (P) is a subjective measure of a person's satisfaction with life. It is measured by a person's answer to the question, "Taking all things together, how happy would you say you are?" As we have already noted, religious people report higher levels of positive emotions than others. A study released in April of 2016 by the Pew Research Center found that 40 percent of highly religious adults—defined as those who "pray every day and attend religious services each week"—consider themselves "very happy," compared with 29 percent of less religious adults. This recent study echoes many others.

Engagement (E) is another word for what some researchers call flow. It is the feeling of becoming so involved in an activity that we lose sense of time. A violinist, for example, enters flow when she is so focused on playing music that she is not distracted by anything else. Engagement means that we cultivate and deploy our strengths in a focused way. These strengths are not always skills. They can also be feelings and emotional commitments. They include the capacity to love, to give, to honor, to be a friend. Faith encourages such pursuits. Indeed, the evidence suggests members of religious communities are more charitable, live longer, and have longer-lasting friendships than those who are not members of such communities.

One of the ways we engage is by building **relationships** (R) with others. Those relationships create a feeling of happiness on their own. They also lead to service. Just think about community service projects you got into because a friend or social group got you to go. You got a chance to experience the satisfaction of helping another person. The impact of such acts on happiness is extraordinary. As Dr. Seligman points out, "Doing a kindness produces the single most reliable momentary increase in well-being of any exercise we have tested."

Meaning (M) is a connection to something we believe is larger than ourselves. It is the part of the PERMA framework most relevant to this book because it is the one most naturally connected with faith. But meaning can be elusive. Sometimes we do not even see it in our lives.

Abraham Lincoln, for example, is one of our great national heroes—and he certainly appeared to live a meaningful life, one that he literally lost in the service of America. And yet, as I recently learned reading a biography of Lincoln, he was plagued with despair. He regularly got lost in the morose thought that his life was meaningless. I was stunned to learn that Lincoln wrestled with this idea, and as I thought about him, I began to realize that meaning involves not only actually giving ourselves to something larger, but also allowing ourselves to notice that we are doing just that. Faith gives us a way to notice how our lives unfold as part of something much larger than ourselves. It gives us a framework with which to notice the meaning of our work. Had Lincoln turned to the perspective of faith, he might have noticed he was living a deeply meaningful life.

Faith also gives us a language and framework for meaning because it puts our lives in a much bigger context than our own limited time and place. Meaning does not fall *exclusively* within the realm of religion. A person who single-mindedly pursues a cure for cancer, for example, brings meaning into their life. But faith provides an accessible avenue wherever and whoever we are.

Accomplishment (A) is another word for *mastery* or *achievement*. It is not winning. It is learning to do something well. Accomplishment can come from woodworking or sailing or playing a musical instrument. It can also come through religious practice. Learning to do a ritual like saying a prayer or a mantra is an accomplishment.

Here's an example. Jews use a variety of melodies for chanting sacred texts. Some of them are quite complicated. One book of the Bible—the book of Esther—requires an intricate melody for chanting the Hebrew that can take many years to learn. A member of my congregation devoted three years to learning how to chant the Hebrew words of Esther to the right melody. He met with a tutor every week. Now he chants it for us every year. The smile on his face when he finishes is priceless.

Of course, PERMA does not capture the whole of happiness. Happiness also involves gratitude, an appreciation for limits, optimism, lifelong learning, and resilience. But PERMA gives us a framework for evaluating our activities and commitments in life.

It also helps us see the extraordinary wisdom embodied in

our Eilu Devarim prayer. As I noted earlier, the prayer guided me through a painful time in my life. Its wisdom brought me back to my community and calling. But the prayer did not change only me. The more I studied it, the more I realized its reach was potentially much wider. It was watching a thirteen-year-old girl struggle through its words that ultimately sparked my commitment to sharing it with you.

This girl was chanting the words of the prayer as part of her Bat Mitzvah service (the Jewish coming-of-age ceremony for girls). She was extremely nervous, and all three hundred people in attendance could tell. She stumbled through the beginning of the prayer. She got stronger toward the middle. By the end she was chanting confidently with a big smile. Then, when she finished, the entire sanctuary broke out in spontaneous applause. This had never happened before.

When everyone quieted, I just started speaking from the heart and saying she had chanted this ancient prayer in Hebrew and inspired us all. I spoke about how powerful the prayer was for me, and then went through each verse and explained the way she could incorporate its lesson into her life. I pulled out the verses in the prayer that addressed the anxiety she'd felt and the exhilarating challenge she'd just overcome. I portrayed its words as a guide to the future challenges she would face. And then I realized why this prayer has been a central part of Jewish tradition for almost two thousand years—it brings our attention to the struggles, actions, and experiences that ultimately bring joy and meaning to our lives. I began referring to it as the happiness prayer. My students started calling it that as well. Soon you will too.

Honor Those Who Gave You Life
כבוד אב ואם

"Feeling gratitude and not expressing it is like wrapping
a present and not giving it."

—William Arthur Ward

A few years ago, a fifty-seven-year-old woman I'll call Ellen
sat in my office. A longtime member of the congregation and
leader in the community, she radiated happiness and success.
We began our meeting with small talk and shared excitement
over upcoming events. She showed me pictures of her daughter,
who was expecting a baby in two months. I shared a few photos
of my two-year-old daughter.

Then the mood changed. Her composure began to fade.
Ellen told me she had not spoken to her own mother in fifteen
years. They'd had a falling out when Ellen divorced and remarried. Ellen told me she hadn't been able to forgive her mother
for the vicious words she had said. She hadn't been able to forgive her mother for the way she had let her suffer financially and
emotionally when she could have helped get Ellen through the
painful divorce.

Then, the week before, Ellen had received a phone call from
her sister, who kept in contact with their mom. The sister told Ellen

their mom had been diagnosed with breast cancer. She would need surgery and radiation. Did Ellen want to get back in touch?

After telling me the story, she looked at me and asked, "Should I?"

I hesitated. I avoid giving specific direction unless it is absolutely warranted. I try to listen more than speak and use what I hear to identify the underlying issues of concern and bring them out into the open. I struggled to figure out the right approach.

"What hesitation do you have in forgiving?" I asked.

"It's not right," Ellen responded. "My life fell apart, and she wasn't there. And we were never really that close to begin with. I could always go to my father. And then the one time I needed her, she wasn't there. How can I love someone like that?"

I thought for a moment. "Do you have to love in order to have a relationship?" I asked.

She paused. She took a deep breath. We sat for about thirty seconds in silence. "I don't know," she finally said.

What It Doesn't Say

Then the answer appeared right in front of me. Behind the couch in my office, where Ellen was sitting, is a sculpture with the Ten Commandments engraved on it in Hebrew. My eyes flitted down to the bottom right-hand corner. In the Hebrew rendering of the Ten Commandments, that corner contains the fifth commandment: "You shall honor your father and mother." In reading those words, I had always focused on the last part of the sentence— "father and mother." I had not given much thought to the verb *to honor*. (I use the phrase *Honor those who gave you life* in my translation so we understand the broader purpose of the verse. The Hebrew literally says, "Honor your father and mother.")

In Hebrew this word is *kavod*. It does not, however, only mean "honor." Biblical Hebrew has only one quarter the number of words of modern English, so many Hebrew words have multiple meanings. One of them is *kavod*. Its other meanings include "heavy" and "weighty." This makes sense. Carrying a weighty object requires significant energy. It demands effort and focus. Honoring a parent can be heavy work.

One meaning *kavod* does *not* have is "love." Our prayer does not tell us to *love* our father and mother. Rather, it tells us to *honor* them. Why? Because God does not ask us to do the impossible. Love of another person cannot be commanded. Love is fickle and demands emotional investment. In an ideal world we would have perfect parents we could love naturally and fully. Our teaching, however, recognizes we do not live in such a world. Some parents are impossible to love. You may be lucky enough to have had perfect parents. Or you may struggle to love. That's OK.

But honoring is different. Honor is what we owe to the people who brought us into life. Honor expresses gratitude for the gift of life itself. Without it we find it difficult to be grateful for anything. That's the logic behind the first prayer Jews say every morning. It is called Modeh Ani. It begins with the words *modeh ani l' fanecha*, meaning "I am thankful to be alive today." We say that prayer every morning even if we feel angry. We say it even if we are in the midst of tragedy. We say it even if we don't believe it at the time. We begin the day with gratitude because life itself is a gift. And just as we honor God with thanks for our lives, we honor our parents because they gave us that gift.

The difficulty comes in figuring out what honoring means. Does it require forgiveness? Does it require financial support? Does it have limits? What if a parent is absent or abusive? The answer differs for each of us, but we find some instruction in remembering two meanings of *kavod*—"heavy" and "weighty." When we honor our father and mother, we cannot bear a load so heavy that we collapse under its weight. Financial responsibilities cannot become so burdensome that we stop taking care of our-selves. Meeting their needs cannot require us to forget our own.

Sometimes honor is simply recognition. We recognize that our parents gave us the gift of life. No matter how we feel toward them, we need to honor the gift of life. Sometimes showing that honor can be extraordinarily difficult. Here's when I saw that most clearly.

Heroes

One late Sunday afternoon I received a call on my cell phone from a local funeral home. The employee asked if I was available to preside over a funeral the following afternoon. The deceased woman (Mary) had been sixty, and the funeral home reported she was survived by two sisters. I agreed to conduct the service, and I called one of the sisters. The phone call lasted two hours.

Mary had grown up in a wealthy family. Her parents had divorced, and she'd had no relationship with her father. She'd succeeded in school and eventually married and had two children of her own. When she was thirty and her two kids were four and six, Mary's mother died. Two months later her grandfather—who had been a father figure to her—also died.

The pain of two consecutive losses triggered depression in Mary. She sought solace in alcohol and partying. One night she went out with two of her children's college-age babysitters. She ended up spending the night with a heroin addict, who took advantage of her drunken and vulnerable state to inject her with a shot of heroin.

When she did not return that evening, Mary's husband began a desperate search. He found her on a street corner four days later. She was addicted to heroin. She refused to return home. She spent the next twenty years on the streets, in jail, and in shelters. Even when she received an inheritance of close to three million dollars, she did not return home. She spent the money on drugs and a lavish lifestyle that lasted about two years. Then it was back to the streets.

She went years without speaking to either of her sisters. She never saw her children. Her husband remarried and moved to a distant suburb. After twenty years she kicked the heroin habit, but replaced it with an addiction to vodka. Aside from ten days living with one of her sisters during the transition, Mary spent the last ten years of her life living on the streets and in a shelter. Then she died from cardiac arrest.

The sister who told me Mary's story had kept up a relationship with Mary's children. They were in their thirties. They had virtually no memories of their mother since they had last really seen her when they were four and six. They thought of her as a shadow and a warning: a shadow cast on their lives, and a warning about the dangers of drugs.

"Did you tell them she died?" I asked the sister. She told me she had. "What did they say when you told them?" I asked. "They said they would see me at the funeral."

I did not sleep well that night. I had to deliver a eulogy and try to make sense of Mary's life. I had to comfort the mourners, but none of them had been particularly close to her. How could I honor Mary's life without denying its tragedy? And what could I say to her children?

The funeral service arrived, and I didn't have any answers. But my answer came when I spoke with her children. I told them how amazed I was at their presence. I gently asked them what had motivated them to come. They told me they had come to the service because Mary was their mom. She'd brought them into the world. She had loved them. The heroin had taken over her life, but it had not changed who she had once been. But they also now knew, they said, about themselves. They saw the ways they protected themselves from strong attachments. They saw some of the real reasons for their conflicts with one another. They saw their vulnerabilities and tendency to avoid risks as reactions to their mom's life. And, to my surprise, they also said they had never felt as grateful as they now did. They felt grateful for their father's role in their lives and for the stepmother who had raised them. They felt grateful for one another. And they felt grateful for the sacrifices others had made for their sake. They knew they'd become the people they were in part because of their mother.

Theirs was an extraordinarily difficult gratitude. But it was also, as they testified, enormously redemptive. They would not have experienced that redemption had they not chosen to honor her. Her daughter captured the paradox of the situation in a remarkable observation. "If she had to choose between getting her next hit and saving my life, she probably would have chosen the hit. But that was not all of her. That did not change the love she had for us."

Honoring Our Parents Helps Us Accept Ourselves

These siblings honored their mother by recognizing her humanity. They could not understand why she'd fallen into the life she did, but they honored her by acknowledging the gift of life she had given them. They honored her by seeing her as she was.

And when we honor our parents as they are, something pro-found happens. We begin to accept ourselves as we are. And we see the blessing alongside the pain. Life itself leaves us in situations like that of Mary's children. Stuff happens to us for no reason. We don't understand why. But honoring the past helps us find some redeeming truth in it. To find the truth, we need to stay in the relationship. And honoring one's father and mother is stay-ing in the relationship. It is not letting go, not giving up, espe-cially when it is easier to do so.

Think of how hard it was for Abraham's son Isaac to find some redemption after his father was ready to kill him. In case you are not familiar with the story from the Bible: Isaac was Abraham's favored son, the one born to his wife Sarah. God had chosen Abraham to be the father of a new nation, and Isaac was supposed to be his successor. Yet, as a test of faith, God asked Abraham to take Isaac to the top of Mount Moriah and offer him as a sacrifice. Abraham obliged and brought Isaac up and prepared to kill him. God stopped him at the last minute. After this harrowing incident, father and son never spoke again. The Bible never records another conversation between them. Yet when Abraham died, Isaac honored him by burying him.

Burying a loved one, as we will see later in the book, is one of the most sacred acts we can perform. It is a way of accompanying a person into the unknown. Death is unfathomable. But when we bury someone, we are doing as much as we can to guide the deceased into that unknown place. Helping bury a loved one is also an act that can never be repaid. If we help out a friend who is moving, for example, we can call that friend up later when we need help. They would likely feel an obligation to repay our favor. That's known by psychologists as the law of reciprocity.

The deceased, however, cannot reciprocate our help. Assisting in burial is an act we perform without expectation of a reward.

Isaac honored his father by burying him. He was joined in this task by his half brother, Ishmael, with whom he had never spoken. Both of them had good reason not to honor their father. Ishmael had been banished by Abraham from their home, and Isaac had almost been killed by Abraham. Many in their situation would have stayed away. I know this because I have officiated at least a dozen funerals where the children of the deceased chose not to attend.

Yet Isaac and Ishmael believed something different. They knew that despite their father's flaws, they owed him their lives. Their burying him was not a sign of friendship or love. We see no evidence Abraham ever apologized for his actions or asked for their forgiveness. Rather, it was a sign of acceptance and recognition. They recognized that Abraham was their father and accepted their responsibility to honor that role.

Then the extraordinary part happens. First, according to some interpretations, Isaac and Ishmael reconciled. The half brothers ended their estrangement from one another. Then Isaac began to develop into his own person. Abraham had cast a large shadow, and Isaac lived under it for the early part of his life. Now we start to hear his voice much more often. He had children. According to the Jewish sages, he instituted the custom of praying three times a day, which traditional Jews still follow today. *Isaac became the leader he was meant to be, but only when he no longer lived under his father's shadow.*

Now, Isaac could have lived with bitter anger at his father. Yet by honoring him, he lifted a weight off his own shoulders. He closed one chapter of his life and began the next. Honoring the past sometimes lets us move out from under its shadow. We carry less baggage as we walk into the future.

How Do We Honor Great Parents?

Isaac needed to distance himself from his father in order to show honor. Sometimes honoring the past involves getting out from under its shadow. Some of us, however, model ourselves after our parents. I am one of these people. As a writer, this occasionally bothers me. An old *New Yorker* cartoon shows a college girl sitting in her dorm room writing a letter to her parents. She writes, "Dear Mom and Dad: Thanks for the happy childhood. You've destroyed any chance I had of becoming a writer." Alas, I hope the joke does not turn out to be true.

Honoring our father and mother may seem easier when we have no doubt our parents deserve such honor. Jewish tradition sets a high bar as to what honoring parents requires. Sometimes it seems as if there is a sliding scale. The more honorable our parents were, the heavier the burden of honoring them. In other words, with privilege comes responsibility.

The Talmud gives us a prime example. In the second century, a rabbi named Tarfon went on a walk with his mother in his garden. As they were walking, Tarfon's mother's foot struck a stone. It broke her sandal in half. As they continued walking, Tarfon knelt and kept his hands stretched under his mother's feet so that she did not have walk barefoot. She walked—and he crawled—in this manner until his mother arrived back at her home a mile away.

Soon thereafter Rabbi Tarfon became ill and his mother stayed at his home. His students came for a visit. When his mother saw them, she asked them to pray for Tarfon because he gave her so much honor. She told them the story of what he had done. They responded by telling her that even if he had done that for her a thousand times, he would not have given her half the honor she was owed.

The absurdity of this closing comment is meant to convey a message. Our mother and father gave us the gift of life. That is a gift that can never truly be repaid. The closest we can come is honoring them. (To be clear, the obligation to honor your father and mother is not simply about biology. It can apply to others who brought you up through the critical years of infancy and childhood.)

I suspect Tarfon's students understood what philosopher Martin Buber called "I–Thou" relationships. An I–Thou relationship is one in which we are closely and personally connected with the other. These kinds of relationships stand in contrast to "I–It" ones, which are functional rather than sacred, conditional rather than eternal. With parents we have an I–Thou relationship. With our cab driver or barista we have an I–It relationship. The wisdom practice of honoring father and mother reminds us not to take these I–Thou relationships for granted.

It is the *uniqueness* of an I–Thou relationship that makes it so strong. Others may try to break or fray it. Accounts from people who became part of a cult frequently recount the cult's efforts to separate new followers from their parents. Parents serve as a symbol of a person's unique identity and past. Membership in the cult is meant to make them a new person beholden to a new leader, whom they might even call Father. To honor our mother and father is to affirm our unique identity and responsibility in the world. It is to show gratitude where it is due. It is to put first things first. It is to give reality a human face. It is to respond to the powerful, intensely personal bonds that created us.

Change as a Form of Gratitude

But even if we had a strong bond with wonderful parents, we may still need to do things differently. We are not always like the son in the Harry Chapin song "Cat's in the Cradle," singing, "I want to be like you, Dad." That song is sung from the perspective of a father watching his son do many of the same things—good and bad—that he did. He has little time for his parents when he is a teenager. Then he works too hard in his career. But eventually he realizes what is most important. He becomes the kind of father that his own dad was. It is a beautiful song. But it's not how many of us live. Sometimes we do honor our parents by repeating their behavior. But sometimes we honor them by doing things differently. Sometimes doing things differently brings honor in ways we cannot imagine.

This idea can be expressed in simple ways. My wife, for example, is never late. If a movie starts at seven thirty p.m., she makes us get there by six forty-five. She is the first in line at school to drop off our kids in the morning. She gets nervous if we are less than two hours early for a flight. It drives me crazy.

We have had endless arguments over this tendency. She knows it borders on the irrational, but she has a good reason for it. Her mom—who worked as an attorney and had a very busy and successful practice—was often late. They always rushed through the airport.

Like her mom, my wife has a demanding career as a rabbi and parent. She got much of that drive and focus from her mom. But she does the opposite when it comes to punctuality. Is this a way of honoring her mom? On the surface, no. But when I ask her about it, she says it is a way of honoring her mom. Her mom did not come late on purpose. She was trying to balance a busy life. Sometimes the balance got thrown off. My wife experienced the brunt of the lack of balance when she had to wait long after other kids were gone.

So, like her mom, my wife strives for balance, but she tries to make it more sustainable. She honors her mom by learning and changing, not by repeating. To learn from the past is to express gratitude for the past. It is to honor its lessons.

My Father

We also honor our parents by learning from the lessons of their lives. But sometimes fear or embarrassment can stop us. As I struggled in my early thirties to lead my congregation, I hesitated to look to my dad for guidance. On the surface it would have made perfect sense to turn to him. I was near the beginning of my career. He was at the end of his. I'd had few leadership experiences. He'd had many. He had so much to teach and was at the age when he wanted to nurture the next generation. Besides all that, I also knew he cared about me more than almost any other person in the world.

But I also wanted to make him proud, and the struggle felt embarrassing. He and my mom had given me every opportunity in life, and I felt I wasn't living up to their expectations. Plus they always seemed to have it together. But the real story turned out to be much different.

It turned out my dad had had many struggles he barely survived. It turned out we had moved from Houston to Milwaukee when I was eleven because of a conflict at my dad's clinic in Houston. But I was insulated from it. My parents made the move when I was away at camp. They wanted to protect me from the difficulties they were going through, and when I arrived in Milwaukee, I jumped right into my new life there. I remember that they even got me a new pair of the world's hottest shoes—Nike Air Jordans—so I would feel more comfortable starting at a new school and fitting in. We didn't really talk about what had happened.

But as we talked about what was going on at the synagogue and about leadership challenges I was experiencing, he opened up more to me. I could tell he wanted to help. Some people make it clear they are not interested in hearing your problems. Have you ever talked to someone you thought might help you, but instead started looking at their watch, or spoke in a tone of voice that indicated they wanted the conversation to end? Well, I got the opposite feeling talking to my dad. When I discussed the difficulties I had counseling congregants going through marital problems and managing a large staff, he asked more questions. Without being intrusive he invited me to go deeper into what I was feeling. And he started to tell me more of his own story.

He'd had a boss who cheated the clinic of significant funds. The shortfall led to layoffs and bad publicity, which threatened his job. He also had to counsel a large immigrant population in Texas that struggled with both language and cultural norms. He and my mom had had to move constantly after he graduated medical school and was serving in the army. Even though I was thirty and long out of the house, I was just learning about my dad's own struggles.

As we talked he not only helped me begin to trust myself and my instincts more, he gave me practical advice drawn from his experience as a therapist and leading a clinic. He even helped me appreciate the happiness prayer more as he talked about the power of meaning in life. As a psychiatrist who served many low-income patients, he frequently had only fifteen minutes to counsel each one. One question he found always helped patients open up was, "What one thing brings you greatest meaning in life?" This question not only helped patients focus on their strengths, it built rapport and helped them feel better about their lives. His insight helped me become a better counselor. It also deepened my appreciation for the way the happiness prayer guides us to find the avenues of meaning in our lives.

I also realized that in seeking my dad's advice I was not only helping myself, I was honoring him. He wanted to be needed. He wanted to share his story. That's something we all want. We want our story to be heard and to matter. My trust in him gave him that. And it gave him honor. When we can give someone an opportunity to make their story matter to others, we honor them.

As a parent of young children, I appreciate even more why this kind of honor matters. I hope my children will honor me in the conventional ways—showing kindness, visiting, expressing gratitude, etc. But I also hope they will honor me in the subtle ways—appreciating my advice, seeking it when it matters, and helping me live my story. This kind of honor is what helps us leave a legacy and sustain values and practices that matter. This legacy adds meaning to our lives and is one of the reasons the sages included honoring parents in our happiness prayer.

It is no accident that this wisdom practice is the only one we also find in the Ten Commandments. The commandment to honor father and mother is the fifth in the Hebrew rendering of the prayer. And it is the only commandment to which there is a reward attached. All the other commandments simply say "Do not..." or "You shall..." Sometimes there is elaboration on what that means, but no reason is given. Except for the fifth commandment. There we read, "Honor your father and mother *so that* you shall long dwell on the land God is giving you" (emphasis mine). In other words, your future as a people depends on honoring those who gave you life. If you honor them, you will survive. If not, you will perish.

The writers of the Bible and the Jewish sages may have intuited one truth revealed by the recently established science of positive psychology. Children who know their parents' and grandparents' histories and stories tend to be healthier and happier than those who do not. Knowing our ancestors' stories is a way we carry their legacy into the future. Honoring them and continuing their stories shows gratitude for the lives they bequeathed to us.

When cultivated effectively, this gratitude extends to other parts of our lives. *Gratitude is the essential ingredient for happiness.* Study after study confirms this truth. One researcher asked people to write down three things they were grateful for every day. After eight weeks they showed significant increases in happiness. Another study had each participant remember someone who had influenced their life, and then contact that person and thank them for what they did. That group also showed significant increases in happiness. The Jewish sages wisely chose honoring the ones who gave us life as the first of our wisdom practices because honor flows out of gratitude. Even if our relationship with our parents has not always been perfect, finding a way to honor them lets us feel more grateful for the gift of life itself.

My Dad's Final Gift

My dad gave me one final gift. He reintroduced me to a book I had read in college but forgotten about. It was Viktor Frankl's *Man's Search for Meaning.* Frankl was a psychiatrist who studied with Freud, but eventually went on to create his own school of thought after surviving the Nazi death camps. *Man's Search for Meaning* tells his story and introduces his philosophy. It was named by the US Library of Congress as one of the ten most influential books of the twentieth century.

Frankl teaches that life is the pursuit of meaning, and we can find redemptive meaning even in our most painful experiences. Those painful experiences can, in fact, help us discover meaning because we need to find some way to survive them. What we find is a clue to what gives our lives meaning. That meaning may be found in a project we still need to complete, or a person for whom we need to survive. The point is that each of us has a purpose only we can serve.

Frankl not only helped me see my struggles as a path to discovering meaning in my life as a rabbi and a writer, he also gave me a deeper appreciation for our first wisdom practice because after rereading *Man's Search for Meaning*, I began to obsess and learn everything I could about Frankl. In one of his biographies, I discovered that Frankl might never have written *Man's Search For Meaning* had he not embraced our first wisdom practice— honoring the ones who gave us life. He exemplified the core lesson of this first wisdom practice: honoring one's father and mother is staying in the relationship. He embraced it at a pivotal moment.

It was the spring of 1941. The Nazis had begun their systematic persecution of Jews. They were destroying shops and synagogues and loading Jews onto trains headed toward the death camps.

Frankl, who lived in Vienna at the time, did not know what to do. He had been granted a visa to go to America. But he had aging parents. They could not move. He knew they soon would be taken by the Nazis and sent to the death camps. And they would likely die without him. He struggled. So one afternoon, to clear his head, he visited St. Stephen's Cathedral in the center of Vienna. As he listened to the organ music, he asked himself, "Should I leave my parents behind? Should I go to America and leave them to their fate?"

He did not hear an answer. Then he walked back to his parents' home. When he sat down at their table, he noticed a piece of marble. His father told him it was rubble from a nearby synagogue that had been destroyed by the Nazis. He picked up the marble. Then he saw, etched on one of its sides, several Hebrew letters. They were the words of the fifth commandment and the first verse of our happiness prayer—"Honor your father and your mother." He had heard his answer. Frankl stayed. And soon he wrote a book that helped millions of people find a reason to keep on living.

Be Kind

גמילות חסדים

"When I was young, I admired clever people. Now that I am old, I admire kind people."
—Rabbi Abraham Joshua Heschel

Imagine if we knew the secret to happy relationships. Imagine if we knew the exact words and actions that would bring peace and happiness. Life would be a lot easier. Parents and children would all get along. Siblings would never fight. Friendships would last forever.

Over the last ten years I've had a front row seat at the creation, maintenance, and occasional breakdown of one particular type of relationship: marriage. Over these ten years I have officiated over five hundred weddings. I do not know how many of them have ended in divorce, but anecdotal evidence suggests about one-third. Perhaps more concerning are the many marriages that fall into bitterness and dysfunction. A recent book, *The Science of Happily Ever After: What Really Matters in the Quest for Enduring Love*, reports that of all the people who get married, only three in ten remain in healthy, happy marriages. That leaves us with a big question: What makes the difference between a happy and an unhappy relationship?

We will never be able to pinpoint a precise answer. As I have often told brides and grooms, *the secret to a happy marriage is that there is no secret*. What works depends on the relationship, and the background and perspective each person brings to it. Yet some key factors stand out. Chief among them is kindness. This truth has been demonstrated repeatedly by the world's foremost marriage researcher, John Gottman. Dr. Gottman has come closest to discovering the secret of happy relationships.

Dr. Gottman oversees a research center known as the Love Lab. For his research he invites couples into the Love Lab and observes them closely over five days. He also monitors their hearts, sweat glands, and blood flow. These measures correlate with feelings of hostility, calmness, and connection. Using the data, he has been able to predict with *90 percent accuracy* which relationships will continue and which will end in divorce. His success in predicting the fates of marriages led him to focus on the practices of the successful couples. What distinguished their relationships?

Successful couples respond to one another's bids. A bid is a verbal or physical invitation to the partner. It invites a response. It includes phrases like "Look at that beautiful bird outside" and "Isn't this a great show?" When we receive a bid, we turn either *toward* or *away* from it. Turning toward a bid shows engagement and interest. It is an act of kindness. Turning away is the opposite. A typical turning away is saying something like "I'm busy."

Couples who were divorced six years after Dr. Gottman observed them had had a 33 percent "turn-toward" bid rate. Couples who were together after six years had had an 87 percent turn-toward bid rate. Kindness makes all the difference. "Kindness," he writes, "glues couples together."

Where Does Kindness Come From?

Now, kindness is not limited to individual relationships. It extends to the way we relate to our families, our communities, our acquaintances, and strangers. We can begin to understand its real meaning by looking at the word itself. *Kind* is related to the word *kin*. Over time, human beings have given special favor to those who are kin, or those who are of our kind. Scientists might say this special attention to our kind gave our ancestors an evolutionary advantage. Kin would watch out for one another, and thereby increase the likelihood of passing on their shared genes.

Over time, however, the Jewish sages—and now modern psychologists—discovered that real kindness encompasses more than kin. It is a way of relating to others. It builds relationships that sustain life and give it meaning. One Jewish commentary on the exile of Adam and Eve from the Garden of Eden says their exile was a positive development in human history because it gave us the opportunity to practice kindness. In the Garden everything was provided for us. Outside it we needed to help one another. Often we resist kindness, and we'll see why later in the chapter. First, however, we need to address the two different types of kindness as understood by Jewish wisdom. In Hebrew they are *chesed* and *rachamim*.

Rachamim refers to acts of mercy. The word derives from the Hebrew word *rechem*, which means "womb." The womb symbolizes nourishment and unequivocal care. Acts of *rachamim* are driven by a desire to give and love unconditionally and unequivocally. I call *rachamim* the Mother Teresa type of kindness. With it we are willing to sacrifice our comfort for the needs of others.

Few of us can consistently perform acts of *rachamim*. They

are rare, and therefore all the more remarkable. But the word *rachamim* reveals the origins of human kindness. It is the mother-child bond. As infants we learn, as writer Adam Phillips puts it, that "our lives depend on kindness...we begin literally of a piece with another's body." As we develop, we need to differentiate ourselves from our parents, and the intensity of the mother-child bond wanes. Yet it is not eliminated, and it eventually finds expression in other relationships. As the Bible pithily puts it, "A man leaves his mother and clings to his wife." Kindness widens from the parent-child bond to other intimate relationships.

Chesed refers to acts of kindness within our other relationships. Those relationships include marriage, friendship, or membership in a community that can be as broad as the planet Earth or as small as a neighborhood block. The point is that *chesed* is a natural part of being in relationships. It expresses our commitment to a particular person or group.

Its rootedness in relationships helps us understand why acts of *chesed* make us happier. We are serving ourselves by serving another, because we are ultimately strengthening the relationship in which we are both invested. As Dr. Gottman discovered, when we turn toward another person's bid, we grow closer. The giver benefits. The recipient benefits. And the bond is strengthened. With *chesed*, one plus one equals three.

Kindness Is Contagious

Kindness is also contagious. When you practice kindness in one relationship—marriage, friendship, parenting—you find yourself, almost magically, naturally inclined to be kind in other relationships. I saw this magic exhibited during a funeral I conducted. The deceased had been a beloved physician. He had been one of those old-time general doctors, always spending time with patients, getting to know their families, and showing a profound caring beyond simply doing the right tests and procedures. His daughter, who had also become a doctor, spoke at the service. She discussed her father's relationship with her mother. She shared a phone call she'd once overheard.

Her mom called her dad at the office to tell him she had gone to the veterinarian. Their cat was sick and in pain. They would have to let her die. She said to him, "I know you're busy, but I really wish you could be home with me for it." He replied, "Honey, I'd come home if you had a hangnail."

This doctor's kindness was not limited to his patients. It was not limited to his spouse. It radiated among them. It touched his daughter and the way she lived. Kindness is rooted in relationships, and one relationship strengthens others. That's part of the beauty of kindness. Unlike money, kindness is never zero sum. You do not lose kindness when you give it away. You get more.

That's something the Jewish sages knew, and that's why they included kindness as one of our ten wisdom practices. We know they understood this nuance of kindness because of the way they phrased this particular wisdom practice. They use the Hebrew phrase *gemilut chasadim. Chasadim* is simply the plural form of *chesed* ("kindnesses" rather than "kindness"). The word *gemilut* is more complex. In Biblical Hebrew *gemilut* conveys reciprocity. The phrase *gemilut chasadim* suggests that when we perform acts of kindness, we get something in return. Being kind to others means we are being kind to ourselves.

Sometimes we can't even imagine what we'll really get from an act of kindness. In 2015 a husband and wife, Simon and Betsy, were visiting Israel from Los Angeles. They stopped at a restaurant in Herzliya, a suburb of Israel's largest city, Tel Aviv, for lunch. They were seated downstairs, but asked to move upstairs so they could enjoy the view. The host agreed. Upstairs they were greeted by a waiter. He told them the specials. As he left, he said, "If you need anything, my name is Barak." Betsy then got a strange feeling in her stomach.

As Barak walked away, she said to her husband, "We have to know his mother's name." Simon felt it was an odd desire, but he did not want to start an argument with his wife at a restaurant in a foreign country. So he asked Barak to come back and said, "I know this is silly, but can you tell us your mother's name?" Barak said it was Orna. Betsy froze. After a few moments she asked Barak, "Did you by chance fight last summer in the war in Gaza?"

"Yes," Barak replied. "How did you know?"

Betsy replied, "Because *I've got your name on my fridge.*"

It turned out that Betsy's niece was a rabbi. During the 2014 war in Gaza, the rabbi told her aunt about a phone number she could call to get the name of an Israeli soldier so she could pray for that soldier and his family. Betsy called the number and received the name Barak bat Orna. (In Hebrew the name literally means "Barak, son of Orna.") So she put the name on her fridge to remind herself to pray for him throughout the war. Even after the war ended, the name stayed on the fridge. Betsy had actually looked at it two weeks before leaving for Israel and thought about him. She did not imagine that she would meet him—this one person—in a country of six million people. This encounter changed them and the many others who heard it by reminding us that kindness and generosity of spirit make miracles possible.

Why Aren't We More Kind?

Here's the question that troubled me when I first read Dr. Gott-man's studies on the power of kindness. If we know kindness is so good for us, what prevents us from being kind more often? Why is kindness not our default response to others? Acts of kindness are sometimes hard to undertake because they are, almost by definition, responses to another person's needs or vul-nerability, and meeting another person's needs reminds us of our own. Responding to others with kindness reminds us that we are never truly self-sufficient—that we too need other people to respond to our own desires and vulnerabilities. And that can make us feel inadequate. As Adam Phillips puts it, "Kindness is always hazardous because it is based on a susceptibility to oth-ers, a capacity to identify with their pleasures and sufferings. Putting oneself in someone else's shoes, as the saying goes, can be very uncomfortable."

A concrete way to picture this is to ask yourself how you feel visiting someone in the hospital. Unless you work in the health-care field, you probably do not relish such a visit. When I visit members of my synagogue, they inevitably tell me that few people outside their family have come to visit. Some ask me why. I tell them that a hospital reminds us of our vulnerabilities. When we visit, we picture ourselves being there. We know it could happen to us. By avoiding it, we feel we somehow protect ourselves.

I feel this way sometimes. I hesitate when getting ready to visit someone in the hospital. I look around and see if there's any other work I can do. But then I remind myself that it is a gift, an opportunity, to get up and go. Visiting someone in need inevitably makes us feel better (not to mention the person we visit). When we share in another's pain, our own vulnerabilities seem slightly less frightening. We not only help salve another's wounds; our own feel less painful.

Suffering as the Root of Kindness

One modern Jewish philosopher, Emmanuel Levinas, used this insight to help explain the religious meaning of suffering. Every human being experiences suffering. No one—not the richest, the most famous, the best-looking—is free from it. It is part of the human condition. Like every spiritual leader, I am constantly asked why. If God is good, and all-powerful, why do we suffer? Thousands of volumes have been written to answer this question. I struggle endlessly with it, especially when officiating at the funerals of children. The only answer I can give honestly is that God suffers alongside us. God's tears accompany our own. I shared this Jewish teaching on Fox News in 2012 right after the horrific school shootings in Newtown, Connecticut. I got hundreds of e-mails in the following days saying this idea brought them comfort. I cannot say it is definitive theological truth. Only God knows the answer to that. But I do know we are not meant to suffer alone. Other people's suffering demands our kindness.

According to Levinas, *suffering is the root of kindness*. Now, Levinas does not say suffering is somehow redemptive or meaningful for the sufferer. A child with a birth defect or severe illness did not do anything to warrant such pain, and to suggest this violates any reasonable moral code. Rather, suffering offers an opportunity for meaning and compassion to the one who *responds* to it. When we answer suffering with kindness, we bring God into the world. We become the hands of God. That is why Levinas called compassion "the supreme ethical principle."

Levinas reshapes the conventional view of kindness. Do you remember that great saying and bumper sticker, "Practice random kindness and senseless acts of beauty"? It came out of the free-for-all spirit of the 1960s. It seems to associate kindness with naïveté, ease, and randomness. But Levinas teaches us that kindness does not come from comfort. It does not emerge out of ease. It is not some random feeling. More often than not, it is a response to pain. It is an answer to struggle. That makes it all the more powerful.

Think of the moments when you or a loved one struggled. Did it make you more empathetic? Did it lead you to feel a deeper connection with others? When my oldest daughter switched schools and struggled to make new friendships in fourth grade, I shared with her the similar struggles I'd experienced when my family moved from Texas to Wisconsin. My wife had never had a struggle like our daughter's. She lived in the same neighborhood and school district her whole childhood. She could sympathize but not really empathize. My struggle gave me a window into my daughter's pain.

The kindness and empathy we give others can help us and them emerge from struggle with a renewed determination to live with greater intention and urgency. An eighteenth-century rabbi captured this truth in a sharp observation. A student once asked him, "How are we supposed to dance at a wedding?" The rabbi answered, "Dance as if you're standing at the edge of an abyss." Life is precarious and struggle is inevitable. We need not respond to that struggle with despair. We can live and love with the intensity of that dance.

What Stops Kindness?

Standing on the edge of an abyss is scary because of the fear it generates. Fear is paralyzing. And kindness generates fear because we expose ourselves to rejection and to loss. Did you ever try to be nice to someone in middle school just to have that person brush you off because you weren't cool enough? Rejection is one of the experiences we human beings strive most to avoid. And it can stop kindness dead in its tracks. It can even transform kindness into anger.

That's a key lesson of one of my favorite novels, Mary Shelley's *Frankenstein*. About a third of the way into the book, Dr. Frankenstein's creature has come to life and gone out into the world. He is roaming through the forest in Switzerland when he comes upon a house inhabited by a blind man. The creature feels kindness toward the man. This good feeling impels him to knock on the door of the cottage and introduce himself. The blind man lets him in. The creature tells him he has been leaving the food and firewood the man and his family have been finding at their door, and they have a pleasant conversation.

Then the man's daughter and son-in-law arrive home. They think the creature is attacking the old man. They scream and go after him with sticks, stones, and furniture, forcing him to flee. His kindness has been repaid with anger. The creature is wounded. He recognizes he will never be accepted, and he determines to take revenge on his creator, Dr. Frankenstein. His is now a life of fury and despair.

Frankenstein's creature experienced the truth of an old quip, "No good deed goes unpunished." But if this were always true, we would avoid acts of kindness. Thankfully, we do not, and they are are not always punished.

For example, we can contrast the rejection of the monster in *Frankenstein* with the compassion shown by the hero of an early twentieth-century Jewish folktale. Once upon a time, a Russian peasant went to visit Moscow, the big city. He arrived at its fanciest hotel. His boots were covered with mud, his clothing was torn, and his appearance was disheveled. Despite all this, the clerk at the hotel smiled at him. He gave the peasant a key to his room, the highest and most elegant room in the hotel. The peasant began walking up the hotel's beautiful winding staircase.

When he arrived at the first floor, he walked right in front of a full-length mirror. He had never seen a mirror before, and he was terrified because it contained a beastly image staring back at him. He growled and shouted at the beast but found it did the same right back to him. He screamed and ran up the next set of stairs. On the second floor he ran into the beast again. He screamed, and the beast screamed back at him. Once again he ran up the stairs, to the third floor. The beast stared right back at him. They exchanged insults and stood toe to toe.

Realizing he could not escape, the peasant ran back down to the lobby. He went back to the clerk at the desk. He told the clerk about the beast stalking him. The clerk quickly realized the man was seeing his own reflection in the mirror. Rather than embarrass or shame him, the clerk told the peasant that the strange-looking man was there to protect the hotel's guests.

"Here's the trick," the clerk says. "If you make an angry face at him, he will do the same to you. But if you greet him with a smile and kind words, he will do the same to you." The peasant thanked the clerk and went up to his room. He had no more terrifying stops.

The clerk could have responded differently. He could have

taken advantage of the peasant's vulnerability and ignorance. Yet he followed Levinas in embracing the ethics of compassion. Another person's humanity was more important to him than a smug sense of superiority. Another person's need gave him an opportunity for kindness.

Without knowing it, the clerk also taught the core truth about kindness this chapter conveys. Kindness is contagious. "If you make an angry face at him," the clerk said, "he will do the same to you. But if you greet him with a smile and kind words, he will do the same to you." Kindness is never limited. The more we give, the more we get. The more we give or respond to another's concern, the happier we become. The way we treat others shapes their happiness and our own.

Kindness is the Heart of Faith

Some of my nonreligious friends often tell me that kindness and religion don't go together. Rather than promoting happiness, they say, religion is the source of all evil in the world. It generates conflict and makes us intolerant of one another. Perhaps you occasionally feel this way. And if you are a person of faith, perhaps friends have challenged you with this accusation.

That is not the religion I teach and know and live. Yes, some people hate in the name of religion. But the deepest impulse of faith is love. It is kindness. It is compassion. It is goodness. And we know faith can motivate extraordinary kindness—and not just the selfless acts of kindness we associate with religious people like Mother Teresa. Faith can show up in the small things we can do every day.

That's the lesson several members of my congregation taught me a few years ago. It was one of the ways their commitment to the happiness prayer infused new vitality and hope into my life. We were about to dedicate a plaque at the synagogue to honor all the volunteers from the past decade, etched with their names and some of the services they had done. I was charged with finding an appropriate spiritual quotation to put in the center. The possibilities were endless, including rabbinic precepts like "Do not separate yourself from the community," and biblical verses like "Build Me a sanctuary so I may dwell among them." I asked myself, "What really draws volunteers to the community? What about this congregation attracts their effort, attention, and resources?"

I decided to ask them. A desire to serve God, of course, was the answer many gave. But so was a simple feeling: The community needed them. Their friends needed them. They could make a difference by bringing a meal to a homebound neighbor or wrapping a gift to send to a soldier on the front lines. A religious congregation often draws out the best in people's hearts. Somehow when a church or synagogue does its job well and invites a loving God into the life of the community, people who walk through its doors are transformed. They take the lessons they learn there and bring them out into the world. What happens in a house of worship has the potential to change us and thereby to change the world. And as we have seen throughout this chapter, it makes us happier.

I found the quotation that captured this sensibility in an obscure section of the Talmud. The Talmud consists of sixty-three volumes of text written in Hebrew and Aramaic. Some people spend a lifetime studying it. Parts of the Talmud are commentary and insights into the Torah and the creation of the world.

But certain sections stand out for their extraordinary power to guide us today. And here is one of them. It is found in the middle of a discussion in which a rabbi is trying to connect two often-overlooked incidents, one near the beginning and one near the end of the Torah (the first five books of the Bible, also known as the Pentateuch). In the first incident—in the third chapter of the book of Genesis—God makes leather garments for Adam and Eve. God clothes them in these garments as they leave the Garden of Eden. Then, near the end of the Torah, in the final chapter of Deuteronomy, Moses ascends to the top of Mount Nebo. He dies there, and God buries him.

The rabbi connects these two incidents by noting that in both instances, God embodies kindness. God clothes and God buries. God protects and God honors. In commenting on these incidents, the rabbi uttered the words I chose for the central quotation of the plaque: "The Torah begins and ends in acts of kindness."

Keep Learning

השכמת בית המדרש שחרית וערבית

"Life is like a ten-speed bike. Most of us have gears we never use."

—Charles M. Schultz

Do you remember experiences when time flew by? You were so engrossed in something that you did not recognize three hours had passed. Maybe it was a book. Maybe it was a conversation or a film. All of us would love more of those experiences. They engage us. They end too soon. How can we have more of them?

The simplest way would be to go back in time. Children have more of these experiences than adults, because their brains are expanding more rapidly. Everything is new for a child. They hear language for the first time, visit a zoo for the first time, and see their first movie. Adults experience fewer such memorable events. We tend to do more repetitive activities. We get comfortable with our routines, our work patterns, our opinions. We notice things less, our brains get more comfortably numb, and the years evaporate. Is there anything we can do to break this pattern?

Aside from discovering a time machine, we can't return to age six or eight. But we can make our adult brains more nimble.

We can recapture some of the joy of new experiences. The secret is learning. When we learn new things—be they ideas, sports, spiritual practices, or physical pursuits—we engage our brains and experience more from life. We can recover the joy of children experiencing things for the first time.

That's the lesson behind our third wisdom practice: keep learning. Too many of us stop learning when formal school ends. Our lives revolve around work, home responsibilities, and other activities. We may learn a few new practices or insights relevant for our jobs, but what about learning for pleasure? What about learning to experience something new? Lifelong learning gives us those opportunities. It may not add years to our life, but it will add life to our years.

The Dangers of Not Learning

Around age twenty-five, a part of the human brain stops growing. It's the part—called the prefrontal cortex—where concentrating and deciding get done. After a while it also starts shrinking. This shrinkage means we take longer to learn something new. The time and effort required lead to resistance. And when we resist learning new things, we miss the joy that comes with it. We don't get the excitement of learning to play the piano. We lose out on the thrill of learning a new language. In resisting that learning, we are sabotaging ourselves. We are missing out on experiences that can make us happier. And the longer we wait, the stronger the resistance becomes. Resisting learning is like avoiding exercise. The longer we avoid it, the harder it is to start.

While the danger may not seem acute, it reveals itself in subtle ways. When we stop learning, we worsen the odds of reaching our potential. We die with our music left inside us. One of my heroes is Rabbi Mordecai Kaplan. Kaplan was the most prolific and influential American Jewish philosopher of the twentieth century. He died in 1983 at age 102. Kaplan made headlines when he conducted the first Bat Mitzvah (Jewish coming-of-age ceremony for girls) in history. Until 1922, when he created the Bat Mitzvah for his daughter Judith, Jewish coming-of-age rituals had been reserved for boys. Kaplan changed that.

He also made long-lasting changes as a Jewish leader. He created community centers for those who had left the synagogue. He wrote dozens of books, several of which are required reading in Jewish seminaries, and left over thirty volumes of diaries.

Kaplan, however, did not write his first book until age forty-one! He was self-conscious about his writing. Having been born in Romania and having immigrated to America at age nine, he did not consider his English good enough to be published. He began by writing short articles. The more he wrote, the better he got. After publishing a few essays, he released his first book. That book—*Judaism as a Civilization: Toward a Reconstruction of American-Jewish Life*—first published in 1934, is still in print in 2017.

Kaplan fought against a widespread belief that our intelligence and creativity peak in our youth. Now, for some people, extraordinary creativity manifests itself at an early age. Mozart and Beethoven were both child prodigies. Albert Einstein did his work on the theory of relativity in his early twenties. But such geniuses are exceptions to the rule. A powerful book entitled *Old Masters and Young Geniuses: The Two Life Cycles of Artistic Creativity* argues that "conceptual innovators"—those like Einstein, who changed our whole view of science—do their best work when they are young. "Experimental innovators"—those like Frank Lloyd Wright and Benjamin Franklin who learn by trial and error and continually invent new things—do their best work later in life.

We can all be "experimental innovators." We can improve on our existing skills, and we can experiment with new pursuits. I read recently about a man in his late fifties who took up tennis. He was drawn to it because his life felt too predictable and boring. He said he wanted something to "counter the looming extended monotonies and unpromising everydayness I imagined awaited me in retirement. I wanted something that did not transpire in my head and at a desk, which is exactly where most of our lives unfold these days. I wanted to learn and get better at something."

Notice that he did not want to get better in order to impress. He did not seek to become a highly ranked tennis player or win a tournament. He wanted the joy that comes from learning and improving. "Am *I* that good? No!" he writes. "I am 63. And I am not really concerned about where all this winds up. It's the getting there I'm enthralled with."

The destination of this journey is a better understanding and appreciation of ourselves. We are like the traveler in T. S. Eliot's poem "Little Gidding": "We shall not cease from exploration / And the end of all our exploring / will be to arrive where we started / And know the place for the first time." Our journey brings us back to our place of origin—our heart and soul. The more we learn, the better we know ourselves. This journey is not always linear. It does not progress neatly and predictably. But every step on the journey brings something new. The more we expand our learning and leave what is familiar, the more varied our steps are. These variations make our lives more memorable and joyful.

What Should We Learn?

OK, you might be thinking: It's important to learn new things, but what should I learn? Schools have curricula. Jobs have requirements. What kind of learning will make me happier?

Well, first we need to recognize that learning in adulthood differs from education in school because of the motivation. For adults, the primary motive is not grades. It is growth. This goal gives us greater flexibility. We can focus on something that both interests us and gives us room to improve. I suggest avoiding areas where you already possess significant knowledge. Try reaching outside your comfort zone. On the other hand, looking for something *connected* to an existing passion can enrich your experience of both the old and the new.

I learned this from my father. He is a jazz fanatic. He has collected records from jazz performers like John Coltrane and Miles Davis for over fifty years. His collection of LPs and compact discs numbers over forty thousand. (He has not yet learned how to use or appreciate iTunes or the iPhone.)

My mom is a singer. She always loved opera, but my dad avoided it. He was interested only in jazz. Yet at age fifty-five he finally gave in to my mom's persistence and attended his first opera. That began a new journey of study, travel, and exploration. They attended classes to understand the languages in which many operas are sung, like Italian. They learned about stagecraft and even read some of the ancient legends on which many operas are based. Appreciating opera helped my dad see jazz in a different way as well. He saw some of the ways it departed from musical traditions and some of the similarities between the themes of classic jazz numbers and those of operatic pieces.

Perhaps you like movies. Maybe you can learn more about

theater and see the ways plays resemble and differ from film. Perhaps you study the Bible. Maybe you can read some of the classic eighteenth- and nineteenth-century American novels that echo biblical themes. Learning something new does not mean we forget something old. Rather, we may well arrive at a new appreciation for what we already know.

Picking something totally outside your comfort zone is more challenging than studying a familiar topic, but potentially more rewarding. I experienced this myself. I was one of those kids who quickly gave up on learning something new if it didn't come easily enough. Sure, I did what I needed to do for school, but I stuck only with the sports and hobbies that came naturally. Singing was something my mom really wanted me to do. She was a performer and also sang in our synagogue choir. When I could not get the right rhythm and tempo easily, I begged to stop. I refused to practice. Finally my mom gave in and let me stop. But now I have started taking lessons again. When I started those lessons, the same feelings of frustration kicked in. But the wisdom and experience of age stopped me from quitting. As adults we can make up for some of what we missed as children. We can explore from a new perspective.

Something That Makes Us Uncomfortable

When I got stuck in my role as a spiritual leader, I realized that I needed to learn something about leadership and organization. Seminary had taught me that the role of the rabbi was teaching, preaching, and counseling. But each one of those areas alone can take up to forty hours a week. And what about nurturing and supervising staff, officiating at funerals and weddings, and working with a board?

So I became a productivity junkie, learning from business leaders like Michael Hyatt and church leaders like Andy Stanley. The business section of the bookstore became one of my main destinations. Much of this process was intimidating and even uncomfortable at first.

A synagogue is not a business. It is not about making a profit. It is about changing lives. I resisted seeing myself as making sales and overseeing a staff. I was way outside my comfort zone. I was more than just intimidated and uncomfortable, I was afraid. What if I wasn't good at it? What if I wasn't cut out to be the leader of a large congregation?

But then I remembered an insight from Michael Hyatt: Fear is usually an indication we are doing something worthwhile. Rather than lead to resistance, fear can invite commitment. It is a sign that we are going in the right direction. So I devoured leadership books. I found the lay leaders in my congregation willing to offer their expertise and experience. The congregation grew as a result. And so did I. I actually found more time to do what I love—preaching and teaching—because the new systems made us more productive and efficient. I'm still not cut out for business. But I saw the way learning something outside my comfort zone could make me better at what I love.

We Can Start at Age Ninety

I was lucky to learn some good business and productivity lessons early in my career. But learning can happen anytime. Abraham was ninety years old when God called to him and started teaching him the basics of the new religion he would oversee! The Jewish sages say Abraham's commitment to growing was one of the reasons God chose him to build a new people and religion.

God knew Abraham would study and teach the new religion to his children. The sages also write that the Bible reveals Abraham's age in order to teach us that we are never too old to learn something new.

But I see in Abraham's story an even more profound truth. Learning sustains our idealism. At age ninety Abraham could start anew. He could muster the spirit to begin a new religion. Learning nurtures our ideals, and ideals keep the human spirit alive. Learning nurtures our ideals by reminding us of what is possible. Sometimes we see age as a barrier. We justify not trying something new because we have "been there and done that." In other words, an advanced age makes it easy to become cynical. We may even spread that cynicism to others. And that's dangerous.

I served as a student rabbi in several small congregations in the South and Midwest during seminary. At each synagogue a pattern would repeat itself. I would meet one of the elders of the congregation. He or she would pull me aside in order to "teach me the ropes." He or she would say, "Look. I know you're learning all this fancy important stuff in seminary. But I'm going to give you the real deal. Most of the men are here because their wives make them come. And the wives are just here to see their friends. So here's what you need to do: just make sure the services aren't too long and that your sermon has a few good jokes."

I suppose these elders meant well. They were trying to help. But they were mistaken. I discovered that the people in the synagogues cared about prayer. They cared about community. And they cared about what I had to say. They could sense if I was going through the motions. And they could sense when idealism shaped the spirit I brought and the words I delivered.

Idealism is not a luxury of the naive. It takes knowledge. It takes persistence. It takes learning. An extraordinary study on happiness showed how true this is. In 1938, researchers began a study of 268 Harvard University students. The research continued for eighty years, focusing on participants' achievements and life satisfaction.

Dr. George Vaillant directed the study for thirty years. He discovered that the happiest people became what he termed "keepers of the meaning." They offered wisdom to those who came after them—children, coworkers, students, and communities—and that wisdom, he wrote, *came from a lifelong love of learning*. They learned from experience. They learned from classes. They learned from travel. And they learned from other people. Their constant learning gave them perspective. It helped them speak about the present with insights from the past. Learning helped them sustain both passion and knowledge.

You don't need to be a Harvard graduate to develop this love of learning. Among the happiest people in my synagogue are a group of forty adults who meet weekly for Bible study. Most of them are in their seventies and eighties. Some went to college and some didn't. Some were doctors. Others were homemakers. Yet they rarely stop talking and exploring the text with enthusiasm and insight. They are the most animated and engaged group in the entire congregation. They prove to me the meaning of an enigmatic Jewish teaching.

This teaching, found in the Talmud, says that every baby in its mother's womb knows the entire Bible by heart. When babies are brought into the world, however, they instantly forget it. All of their life is a journey to recovering it. All of life is a quest to return to the ancient wisdom we once knew by heart. The older we become and the more consistent we are in our learning, the closer we come to attaining that perfect knowledge we once had. In other words, learning is a journey of both *progress toward* and *return to* our best selves.

Learning to Know Ourselves

Three thousand years ago Socrates also said that learning is a form of self-discovery. Embracing this perspective not only helps us discover our passions and enrich our relationships but can help us find a way to thrive through life's setbacks.

In my congregation there was once an extraordinarily successful real estate developer and art collector. He had more trappings of external success than anyone I knew. Yet when he was in his eighties, a series of events upended his life, and he asked me to study with him to help him through them. First he learned he had been adopted. Then he met his twin brother, who turned out to live less than a mile away. In fact, the twin brother had once visited this man's home for a social event, not knowing, of course, that the owner of the home was his twin!

The events shook his sense of self, and we met regularly for lunch to study and discuss some biblical and Talmudic texts. The sessions were fascinating because his mind brimmed with insights and connections between the texts and literature, art, and so much more. Frequently we would veer off into more personal issues.

Once I gently asked him what had brought him to the study of Jewish texts. Sure, he'd had some life upheavals, but he had never really been that interested in his Jewish religion, and he'd rarely attended synagogue. He could have been doing so much else. He could have been studying art more deeply. He could have gone into regular psychoanalysis. His answer? "Rabbi, only through these words can I understand who I am." That is learning at its best.

Harnessing the Brain to Ask the Right Questions

This man knew the core questions to ask. Some of us still struggle. We ruminate throughout the day and night. Unfortunately, much of this rumination is negative self-talk. We criticize and dwell on what we said and what we think we should have said. We imagine what others are thinking about us. This rumination is not productive.

Focused learning is a way to redirect our brains. We can take the energy required for ruminating and direct it to something that adds to our happiness. I've learned an extraordinary technique for doing so. It is called "cognitive reappraisal."

First we write down our ruminations. Writing them down externalizes them. It gives them contours and gets them out of our head so we can look at them objectively. Then we determine their triggers. What sparks these negative thoughts? Does a certain person or activity trigger them? We write down those triggers. Then we ask ourselves about the feelings sparked by those triggers. Do we feel inadequate or intimidated or unintelligent?

Once we have written down these triggers and feelings, we look objectively at them. We look for evidence for their lack of validity. Let's say we wrote down, "Small talk makes me anxious because I am bad at it." Our next step would be to ask ourselves whether we are really that bad at small talk. We look for counterexamples. We might say to ourselves, "What about the meeting I had last week with a new coworker? I didn't worry about small talk. We just chatted."

After we have questioned our triggers, we can figure out ways to counter them. We might say to ourselves, "I don't have to be perfect at small talk in order to do my job well." Or we can say, "I am good enough at small talk to form the relationships I need to succeed." We are questioning our ruminations and replacing them with positive observations. The goal is not to trick ourselves. It is to see ourselves more accurately. That's why scientists call it cognitive reappraisal. We are looking at ourselves from a different perspective. We are learning to reappraise ourselves.

Over time this reappraisal becomes a habit. We create a new neural pathway in our brains. We study ourselves in order to change ourselves. We go outside ourselves in order to empathize with ourselves. And it works. In 2014 a study showed that people who practiced cognitive reappraisal over sixteen weeks significantly reduced their negative emotions. Happiness begins in the mind. Consistent learning helps us use our minds more effectively.

A Big Lie We Sometimes Believe

The practice of cognitive reappraisal not only makes us happier but also reminds us that we can grow as individuals. One of the great barriers to lifelong learning is the idea that intelligence is relatively fixed. This idea is reinforced by the emphasis placed by schools on standardized tests. It is reinforced by various personality tests that label us as "introverts" or "intuitives." Such tests are not all bad. They can help illuminate parts of ourselves. (I learned from taking an Enneagram test that I am equal parts "achiever" and "helper.") But these tests can become dangerous when we see them as purely descriptive rather than instructive.

Our character is not captured by a series of standardized questions. It is shaped by our learning and growth. If we say our intelligence and character are frozen, we might as well say our happiness can't be changed. But dozens of studies prove otherwise. Our well-being tends to improve over time. The more we learn, the more we grow, and the happier we become. As we experience and draw insights from the world, we learn who we really are.

As a seminary student I became intrigued by a man who lived this truth in a powerful way. His name was Franz Rosenzweig. He had been born in Germany near the end of the nineteenth century. This was an interesting time for German Jews because many universities and professions were open to them, but social shunning of Jews still prevailed. Rosenzweig was an academic prodigy, and was fortunate enough to have parents who sent him to the best schools. He earned a doctorate in philosophy and planned to become a professor. Yet while the top universities would accept Jews as students, they would not invite them to become tenured professors.

At first Rosenzweig did not mind. While he had Jewish parents, Rosenzweig had never practiced his religion, and several members of his extended family had been baptized. He was ready to leave his faith. Yet, as a good philosopher, he decided to investigate Judaism so he could make a thorough and thoughtful choice about whether to stay in it or leave it. He determined to learn all he could.

As part of his process of learning, he attended a Kol Nidre worship service. Kol Nidre means "all our vows." The service begins the most sacred Jewish holy day, Yom Kippur, the Day of Atonement.

Rosenzweig had never attended a Kol Nidre service before that night. It transformed his life. He abandoned his plans to become a philosophy professor. He began studying Judaism with Martin Buber. And soon he served in the German Army during the First World War. From the front lines he sent postcards to his mother. His mother took the often-torn postcards and copied their messages onto paper. The postcards became his most celebrated book, *The Star of Redemption*.

One of the arguments of the book is that God reveals himself to every individual in the here and now. God is not a being who spoke only in the past. We can *still* hear God's voice if we listen carefully. Learning, according to Rosenzweig, begins one's return to God. It is the first step on the road back to happiness because it opens up our ears and hearts. What each individual needs to hear and learn is unique. It depends on background and temperament. But the learning begins when we take the first step.

Rosenzweig applied this philosophy to his teaching. In 1920 he began a school called the Lehrhaus. The title speaks to its mission. Lehrhaus means "house of learning," and it is a standard German translation of the Hebrew term *beit midrash*, "house of study." In his school Rosenzweig began where the students began. He helped them take the first step. He did not teach to impart information. He taught to change lives.

Rosenzweig's approach to Jewish learning was like the approach of positive psychology: he sought to strengthen the individual and build upon his life experiences so he could see his life in a new and sacred context. This approach spoke to many caught in the rising tide of anti-Semitism in 1930s Germany. Soon after Rosenzweig's school opened, Hitler made his first public speech and the Nazi Party began to gain strength. The number of students at the school rose as learning became a way to build community and find hope and comfort in Jewish tradition, a way to enhance lives and cope with the sharp rise in persecution. Some of the Jews who escaped from Nazi Germany—people like Rabbi Abraham Joshua Heschel—had been students or teachers at Rosenzweig's school, and they credited their experience at the school with giving them hope and fellowship in a time of despair.

Rosenzweig's own life demonstrated the power of his teachings. In 1921 he was diagnosed with amyotrophic lateral sclerosis or ALS, which we now call Lou Gehrig's disease. He gradually lost his ability to write, and his speech was significantly impaired. In 1923 he began using a special typewriter that allowed him to push a lever to a disk on the desired letter. Eventually, as his strength diminished, his wife began moving the lever for him, often guessing the word after he had indicated the first letter.

Despite his pain and disability, Rosenzweig continued to write and receive visitors. In fact, he and Martin Buber began a translation of the Bible in which they sought not simply to capture the literal meaning of the Hebrew, but also to convey a sense of its mystery, rhythm, and spoken quality. While incomplete, this translation inspired many future translators, including Eugene H. Peterson, who edited *The Message: The Bible in Contemporary Language*.

Rosenzweig demonstrated the way a thirst for learning and growth sustains one through difficult times. As he taught and wrote, he knew his life had ultimate value.

You may still be in the early stages of finding your life's passion and need to experiment with different pursuits. But one day something will spark your love and commitment, as happened to Rosenzweig. And learning will become a joy and source of strength.

A Countercultural Power in Learning

Rosenzweig was convinced learning was about more than acquiring skills and making a living. It was about knowing ourselves and finding meaning in our lives. This vision is a countercultural one today. We live in an era of pragmatism. We live in era in which some magazines rank colleges based on how much money the average graduate earns. But the most powerful and transformative learning helps us reach deeper goals. It develops our ideals and builds our character. It helps us know ourselves so that we can find the meaning and happiness that are uniquely ours.

The most important aspect of learning is captured in the ancient Jewish custom of giving three-year-old students a taste of honey as they begin their biblical studies. The message is that learning is sweet. Learning makes our lives richer and more fulfilling. Learning is not only about developing new skills. It is about developing ourselves.

That explains why reading novels is a form of learning. As part of a happiness curriculum I developed for a synagogue class, I assigned the great novel *The Remains of the Day*. It challenges us to live with fewer regrets by revealing the painful life of its lead character, the butler Stevens. Most of the other readings for the class were essays in psychology and Jewish philosophy, and this novel generated some pushback. One student told me that she read only nonfiction, and asked me, "Why should we read any fiction? We don't learn anything from it." She wanted us to read more books about Jewish history. I love history books, and I told her so. But I also suggested that good novels reveal parts of the human condition—our hopes, our conflicts, our confusion, our ambitions, our possibilities—in ways nonfiction usually doesn't.

This exposure adds to our emotional repertoire and ability to empathize, helping us relate to others and making us happier.

Ultimately we learn so that we grow. The world needs us to grow because the world needs our unique voices. I encountered this truth most poignantly in Dwight Eisenhower's autobiography. He talks about hearing his mother say that every child needs to be raised to believe that without them their family would fall apart. It would be incomplete.

The implications of this observation hit me sharply. What if each of us believed that the world as we knew it could not exist without us? What if we knew we brought a unique light into the world that it so needed? Eisenhower knew the world needed him. It expected something from him, as it does from all of us. Learning helps uncover what that is. It helps us discern what is inside us. And with that knowledge we grow happier because we are doing what brings us meaning.

Invite Others into Your Life
הכנסת אורחים

"We are not meant simply to invite people into our homes, but also to invite them into our lives. Having guests and visitors, if we do it right, is not an imposition, because we are not meant to rearrange our lives for our guests—we are meant to invite our guests to enter into our lives as they are."

—Lauren F. Winner

In learning about ourselves, we discover that we cannot fully become ourselves all alone. We need other people. We need to invite them into our lives.

How did you become the person you are? Was it through particular experiences at home? Was it through mentors and teachers who guided and inspired you?

I decided to become a rabbi at the dinner table. It was not my own or my parents'; it was the table of a college professor. At the time (the late 1990s) Professor Arnold M. Eisen taught at Stanford University. I met him during sophomore year, when a roommate persuaded me to take his course Jews and Judaism in America. Jewish studies classes were not on my radar. Law school beckoned, as did a potential PhD in American history. I figured the Jewish studies classes would be a good opportunity to meet girls, and probably make my parents and grandparents happy. But an intellectual feast and personal transformation followed.

The intellectual feast took place in the classroom and office hours. I saw a depth in Jewish learning I'd never witnessed before, even though I had attended Jewish day school. But the personal transformation took place at Professor Eisen's home. And it was far deeper.

It began with an invitation to a Sabbath dinner. In Judaism the Sabbath begins Friday evening. Some families go to the synagogue for worship. Others enjoy a festive meal and linger around the table with family and friends. That describes Professor Eisen and his family.

At his home, conversation focused on ideas, books, history, and the Bible. Political and business matters were forbidden. Professor Eisen would often pose a tough biblical question, give us some context, and invite all of us to discuss. Those present included his teenage children, who seemed to relish the gathering; other undergraduate students; his wife, who was also a Jewish studies professor; graduate students in philosophy and religious studies; and other friends and family.

The children, in fact, followed a rule. They were not allowed to go out with friends on the evening of the Sabbath, but they could invite any friends over to the home. So the company was large and eclectic.

I was intimidated at first, but the comfortable atmosphere—one in which grades were not passed out and no one asked if the topic was going to be on the final—gave me confidence. Even though I had grown up in a proudly Jewish home, Sabbath dinners were not something our family did. Judaism was something that happened for me primarily at the synagogue and at school. Professor Eisen showed me the way it happened at home.

He also saw something in me that I did not yet see in myself. He saw in my questions a desire not only to learn the texts and ideas we studied, but also to understand how I could find deeper meaning and satisfaction in life. He saw a college student searching for wisdom and direction, and he responded by welcoming me into his home and family. He taught me that Judaism is not just a religion of the head. It is also one of the *heart*. I was searching, and I needed a guide. Professor Eisen was that for me.

He followed in the tradition of the greatest personalities of the Bible. They did not simply teach, they also modeled the wisdom practice of *hachnasat orchim*. The phrase means "welcoming guests." This translation does not, however, do justice to the force of the Hebrew words. For the Jewish sages, welcoming guests was not just a nice thing to do. It was not simply a display of good manners. It was not even something one did because one wanted to be a good role model for one's children or community.

Hospitality should be a way of life, a thread running through our days. The sages captured this truth in a Talmudic law. They decreed that every home needed to have a door on each of its four sides so guests would have no hassle coming in. Their concern was not for the decor inside the home. It was not for the landscaping or the architecture of the home. Their concern was that a homeowner should not make it too difficult for people to visit.

Can you imagine such a practice today? Today, as cultural anthropologists have pointed out, we tend to spend our time in the backyard rather than on the front porch. The backyard is more private and is frequently fenced in. It does not lend itself to the casual conversation and openness of the front porch. But our prayer tells us to be front-porch people. Rather than turn our home into a fortress, we should turn it into an oasis, a place of conversation and kindness.

Ultimately hospitality is a path to happiness and holiness. The happiness comes from experiencing others. And the way we treat others, as we shall see throughout this chapter, determines who we become.

The holiness comes from our modeling of God. God created this world and invited us to live in it. We can do no less for one another. This chapter explores ways we can do so as individuals, as families, and as communities, and how each act of hospitality adds to our feeling of well-being.

What Kind of Person Are You?

Hospitality begins with people. It rests on the idea that we are not alone. We are, as the Jewish sage Maimonides put it, social animals. But so are other animals. Ants stay together because they are programmed to do so. Many animals travel in packs for security. Human practices of hospitality probably originated in a similar desire for security. Consider the desert traveler who comes upon a tent and is offered life-giving water. Hospitality can be the difference between life and death.

Faith, however, has a way of taking natural human instincts and practices and transforming them into something sacred and meaningful. Eating, for example, is something we all do. We do it to survive. A faith perspective, however, sees eating as a holy act. We sanctify it with grace, conversation, and artistry. We transform a biological necessity into an expression of creativity and a source of meaning.

We do the same when it comes to hospitality. Food *sustains* our life. Hospitality *gives meaning* to life. The two work in concert with one another. The central biblical examples of this truth are Abraham and Sarah.

In a pivotal scene in Genesis 22, Abraham is standing at the entrance to his tent. The sages suggest he always stood at the entrance to the tent so he could see visitors and prepare to welcome them. He does just that when he sees three men walking toward the tent. When he sees them, he rushes inside and asks Sarah to prepare some food.

When the men arrive, Abraham greets them warmly. He offers them water. He washes their feet. He serves them a meal. He shows them *kavod*, a word we explored earlier, which means "honor" and "dignity." His extraordinary hospitality is possible in part because he was standing at the entrance of his tent, anticipating visitors. He might have missed them had he not been waiting eagerly for them.

Entertaining Angels Unawares

What Abraham and Sarah do not realize is that the men are angels. That is the origin of the famous phrase in the book of Hebrews that sometimes we "entertain angels unawares." These angels come to tell Abraham that Sarah will soon bear a child. One wonders when reading the story whether they would have delivered such news if Abraham and Sarah had not offered them hospitality. Their arrival may have been a test of sorts, one in which the couple's behavior toward the guests determined whether they would merit the news the angels ultimately deliver. Whatever the case, we know their arrival brings joy to Abraham and Sarah. Had they not welcomed the strangers, they would not have had cause to rejoice.

Part of the power of the story comes from Abraham and Sarah's ignorance of the identity of their guests. They do not know they are angels. The lesson here is that the status of our guests should not matter to us. Hospitality is primarily about *how* we welcome, not *whom* we welcome. This lesson recurs throughout the Bible.

The fourth chapter of 2 Kings, for example, tells of a woman who saw a stranger in town and urged him to come to her home and eat. From then on he would stay there when he was passing through. The hosts built a room atop their home where he could stay whenever he visited. They furnished it with a bed, lamp, table, and chairs. It turned out their visitor was a prophet named Elisha. He eventually expressed his gratitude and asked the woman what she wanted. She asked for nothing. Elisha soon discovered, however, that she wanted a son, but was unable to conceive. Elisha performed a miracle, and the woman and her husband had a baby boy.

A few years later, however, the boy died. The despondent mother visited Elisha. She chided him for promising her a son and delivering on the promise, but then letting the boy die. She reminded him she had not requested his help. Elisha was the one who had initiated the miracle. The woman was telling the prophet that she would rather have never been given a son than to have been given one, as she had, and then lost him prematurely. The prophet understood, and he followed the woman home. He brought the boy back to life.

When we look at the story as a whole, we see, once again, an act of hospitality ultimately leading to a miracle. We see an illustration of the extraordinary possibilities that arise when we welcome others into our lives. *We never know the ultimate consequences of the hospitality we offer.*

Hospitality has another side benefit. It helps us *remain open to life's possibilities*. Neither Sarah nor the woman from 2 Kings believed she would have a child. Their hospitality, however, invited new possibilities into their lives. They opened the doors to their dreams.

Think about times in your life when an act of hospitality or simply welcoming somebody new into your life achieved an unanticipated result. It need not even have come from an explicit act of hospitality. *Hospitality is a mind-set as well as a set of actions*. It is a mind-set that embraces the possibilities that come from encounters with other people. Such encounters change our lives.

One couple I married recently told me about the party where they'd met. Neither one of them had wanted to go. Yet both of them had good friends who pleaded with them to do so. The friends said they might meet someone there. So they reluctantly agreed. And this act of friendship, fueled by an openness to life's possibilities, led them to meet their life partner.

What Hospitality Can Bring

Something similar happened to me eight years ago. I already had my life partner. But I found my spiritual home. A friend invited me to have dinner and attend a lecture out in the Chicago suburbs. I worked downtown at the time, serving as the assistant rabbi of a large congregation. It was a weekday, and driving out to the suburbs would take two hours. My friend pushed and pushed, and even agreed to treat me to dinner at my favorite suburban restaurant.

The lecture took place at a synagogue called Solel, and it told the story of the congregation's commitment to the community.

Martin Luther King Jr. had spoken from the synagogue's pulpit. Members had marched in Selma and Washington, D.C. As a young rabbi, I was searching for a place that would support and nurture my passions. I fell in love.

A year later one of its leaders reached out to me because the congregation was searching for a rabbi. A year after that I became the rabbi of Congregation Solel, where I continue to serve. The challenges I felt there led me to discover the happiness prayer, which has guided my leadership and increased my faith. It all started with an act of hospitality. Hospitality is not something that happens only at one's house. It can take place at one's spiritual home. And it is not simply a set of behaviors. It is an openness to the opportunities life presents us.

Openness is more than attitude. It is a core personality trait. It is one we can cultivate. And it is one of the five traits captured in the acronym OCEAN, which stands for openness to experience, conscientiousness, extraversion, agreeableness, and neuroticism. Each of these traits has multiple expressions, and each of them is an important part of the quest for happiness. Openness to experience, however, is the one linked most directly to it.

To see why this is true, we need turn to the Jewish holiday of Sukkot. Sukkot is a holiday in which we live in a temporary dwelling place—called a sukkah—that is made from wood beams and covered by various agricultural products.

At least one side must be *open*, and the covering of the sukkah has to have enough *openings* that a person in the sukkah can see the stars in the sky. Jews commit to eating their meals and (if physically possible) sleeping in the sukkah for eight days. This tradition reminds us of the forty years the Israelites spent living in temporary dwellings in the wilderness. They were exposed to the elements. They were not insulated from one another. They depended on one another and on God. For eight days every year we live in the same way.

One might think Sukkot is a difficult holiday. We have to live outside. We have to worry about bugs, rain, itchy grass. Yet Sukkot is the only holiday described in the Bible as *zeman simchataynu*, "a time of happiness"! The time we spend living in the sukkah—in an open, exposed environment with only God and one another to depend on—is the happiest time of the year. It is a time of "complete joy." Two important factors make it so full of happiness.

The first was captured eloquently by my colleague Rabbi Joel Padowitz. In describing sukkahs, he calls them "flimsy huts furnished with little more than plastic chairs and foam mattresses." Yet, he asks, "What better place could there be to remind ourselves that true happiness comes not from all the stuff we have, but from what we still have when stripped of all our stuff?" This message challenges the prevailing culture. Commercials tell us we need this car or this phone in order to be happy or satisfied. They encourage us to depend on things we possess as our source of identity and well-being.

Sukkot tells us something different. It tells us our greatest happiness comes from the times when we focus on people rather than things. When we focus on our possessions, we always think about getting more and more. As the book of Ecclesiastes, which is traditionally read on Sukkot, puts it, "Water fills the sea, but the sea is never full." *We can fill our homes with things, but they will never fill us.* Instead, on Sukkot, we focus on the essentials of life. Those essentials are the people with whom we share life, and the God who gave it to us. We discover God not through buying more things, but through giving, studying, and loving. That is the path to ultimate happiness.

Jewish tradition goes even further in embodying this truth. In addition to living in the sukkah, we are commanded to invite guests to join us in it. Why? Because extending hospitality is a way of fulfilling the imperative to experience total joy on Sukkot.

Even more interesting is the way we welcome guests. When we invite people over, we usually try to create the most comfortable environment. We serve our finest food and use our best silverware. In my home, inviting people over forces us to clean up the house. And we show respect to guests by offering them our best.

But Sukkot is different. The sukkah is deliberately simple. Hospitality on Sukkot is like inviting friends over to hang out in your tent. Somehow these circumstances make us happier. The reason is the feeling of interdependence it fosters. Our most memorable and exciting times often come out of uncomfortable situations. Think about the experiences that challenged you most. You probably remember them more than you remember the predictable times.

The Limits of Openness

Now, openness has some limits. Openness does not mean anything goes. We all need boundaries. We cannot let everyone and everything into our lives at any time. Without some set of boundaries, openness would diminish our own identities. In other words, if guests were with us all the time, we would never know the meaning of family. And sometimes openness can be an avoidance of intimacy. But for the Jewish sages, openness and intimacy complimented one another. Close relationships and openness to others can exist simultaneously. And what we learn from others can deepen our appreciation of our own experiences, and make us more aware of the beauty and diversity around us.

My friend Michael Hyatt tells the story of a time he, his wife, and their five daughters went camping. It ended up getting very cold and they couldn't get their tent up properly. They seemed destined to an evening of freezing in the bitter cold or hiking in the dark back to their car. They ended up meeting another family, finding a new site, huddling close, and having one of their most memorable experiences. He says his family remembers this vacation more fondly than their trip to a fancy resort in Hawaii.

We human beings are made to work together. Think about the creation of the world in the opening chapters of the Bible. For the first few days, everything is good. The waters, the vegetation, the plants, and the sky—all of them God proclaims "good." The first negative note is introduced when God says, "it is *not good* for man to be alone" (emphasis mine). To be totally independent—separate from every other human being—is the first thing described as "not good." We become truly human when we are with others. That's how we were created and how we evolved. When we experience that interdependence, we feel like ourselves. We feel what the Jewish sages call *shalom*, a fullness and completion in one another.

To achieve that feeling, we give *and* receive. We welcome guests into our sukkah, and we enter the sukkahs of others. We give and receive, and by doing so we enrich one another. Rabbi Larry Kushner captured this truth in a striking metaphor: "Each lifetime is...a jigsaw puzzle. For some there are more pieces. For others, the puzzle is more difficult to assemble....But know this. No one has within them all the pieces.... Everyone carries within...at least one...piece to someone else's puzzle." Happiness comes during the times when we put those pieces together.

You Are Never Alone

Hospitality teaches interdependence. It teaches openness. Underlying both these values, however, is a deeper truth. Things do not bring happiness. People do. Happiness is more of a *who* than a *what*. All the possessions we have and the pleasures we pursue are ultimately distractions from what brings us the greatest joy: the relationships we nurture. That is the underlying message we find in the biblical book we read in the sukkah—the book of Ecclesiastes.

On the surface, Ecclesiastes and Sukkot seem to go together like oil and water. Sukkot is all about joy. Ecclesiastes tends to despair. Sukkot happens in the fall, as the leaves are changing and beauty surrounds us. Ecclesiastes emphasizes how mundane the seasons are. Put simply, Sukkot seems joyful; Ecclesiastes is rather depressing.

What I discovered when studying Ecclesiastes in depth, however, is that the book and holiday complement one another. Sukkot is the response to the lessons of Ecclesiastes. Ecclesiastes tells us what happiness is not. Sukkot shows us what it is. When we learn from Ecclesiastes what happiness is not, we see how critical the lessons of hospitality embedded in Sukkot are.

According to Ecclesiastes, we often think of happiness as pleasure. Another word would be *hedonism*. The more wine we drink, the more tasty foods we consume, the more things we buy, the happier we will be. That is the initial assumption of the author of Ecclesiastes, traditionally thought to be King Solomon, the wisest man in the world. The book of Ecclesiastes reflects his journey to that wisdom. He began that journey by acknowledging the difficulties of life. We experience pain, loss, and frustration. How then, he asked, do we find happiness?

His first hypothesis was that pleasure was the answer. The phrase *Eat, drink, and be merry* comes from Ecclesiastes. This pursuit, however, simply does not work. The pleasure is temporary. After the drink wears off, the sadness remains.

Solomon then tried a second pursuit. He decided to accumulate enormous wealth. He built mansions, plants vineyards, and hired thousands of servants and concubines. He "has more than any other man." And what was the result? His unhappiness remained. He felt as if he were pursuing a phantom. Our possessions become a distraction, not a solution. They can even magnify our unhappiness. I imagine Solomon looking around at all his possessions and getting more depressed, saying to himself, "Even with all this, I am still unhappy. Nothing can help me."

Science has proven what King Solomon suggested. Study after study suggests that once basic needs have been met, wealth does not increase happiness. The reason is that more money changes our baseline for happiness. Where we once might have found happiness in a used Toyota, if we make more money, we think we need to buy a Lexus. If we have a Lexus, we think we need the fully loaded model. And so on. The escalation never ends.

This human flow is actually rooted in one of our strengths. We human beings are extremely resilient, as we will talk about later in the book in the chapter "Celebrate Good Times" on page 104. We can adapt to different circumstances. We can look at what happened to us and say, "It could be worse." That same ability to adapt, however, hurts us when it comes to the search for happiness. We look at what happens to us and say, "It could always be better." In other words, when it comes to money, our feeling of happiness is relative. We feel better if we make more than those around us. Some studies even suggest that when it comes to very high levels of wealth—the upper half of the 1 percent—happiness decreases. A successful rap artist once put it simply: "Mo Money Mo Problems." The author of Ecclesiastes figured this out 2,500 years ago.

Why Tim Ferriss Is Wrong

Even after arriving at this understanding, Solomon persisted in looking for happiness. He figured that if hedonism did not work and wealth did not work, perhaps stoicism would. Perhaps a feeling of detachment—of holding oneself apart from the emotions of the masses—would lead to happiness. A variant of this point of view predominates among some Buddhists today. Accept the suffering of the world. Try to live with a loving detachment. Meditate and clear your head. Do not let the troubles of the world affect your core being.

Some thinkers today even advocate a modern embrace of Stoicism. Tim Ferriss, a popular author for millennials and technology enthusiasts who wrote the international best-seller *The 4-Hour Workweek*, also edited a book called *The Tao of Seneca: Practical Letters from a Stoic Master*. Seneca is one of the founders of Stoicism, and he urged a courageous acceptance of the tragedy of the world. In such a world, we accept that bad things happen for no apparent reason. We expect no ultimate justice, nor do we hope for it. We resign ourselves to the world as it is, with no yearning to create the world as it ought to be. This resignation frees us from the burden of responsibility to society or future generations.

This Stoicism, however, is a sophisticated form of escape. Detaching oneself from the world does not bring happiness. It brings only further despair. According to Solomon, those who simply accept the cruelty of the world "don't find rest." Their route "is pointless."

So what, then, does King Solomon discover about happiness? Why do Jews read his book during the holiday on which we are commanded to be happy? He discovers that happiness depends on faith. The path he finally settles on is "Fear God and follow His commandments." Now, the Hebrew word we translate as "fear" means much more than fear in the physical or psychological sense. It means "awe" or "wonder." The verse could well be translated, "Stand in awe and wonder at God's universe, and follow the lessons you have been taught." This closing line from Ecclesiastes captures the meaning of faith for anyone—not just Jews or Christians. It simply asks us to live for something larger than ourselves and follow the basic practices that arise from such a perspective.

For Solomon, faith is self-transcendence. It is living with and for others. That's why we read it on Sukkot, a holiday celebrating hospitality. The sukkah itself is a symbol of faith. The roof needs to have enough openings that we can see the sky above us. The opening of the sukkah remains wide so we can welcome those around us. The temporary nature of the sukkah reminds us that we are temporal inhabitants here on Earth. Our permanence rests in God and one another. Happiness is never something we find all alone. It comes from sharing what God has given us.

Ultimately that is the message the book of Ecclesiastes is trying to convey. Scholars have noted that the biblical book itself uses the word *hevel*, which means "vanity" or "futility," forty times. But it also uses the word *simcha*, or "happiness," seventeen times. That's more times than the five books of Moses put together! All of the book's meditations on futility end with exhortations to happiness. And as we know from the conclusion of the book, happiness is found through faith in God and in one another. The kind of faith Solomon portrays is not a narrow, sectarian one. It does not prescribe what one must believe about God. It does not prescribe the prayers one must say. It simply says happiness comes from the faith that connects us to one another.

Bringing Heaven Down to Earth

Hospitality is something faith can nurture. The Hebrew Bible instructs us thirty-six times to welcome the stranger. It tells us only once to love our neighbor. Perhaps God recognized that it is easier to love our neighbor than to love the stranger. Hospitality, in other words, needs to extend to those who are different from us. If it doesn't, our faith is incomplete.

That's why Jewish law says a person should not visit the house of study unless he has a guest staying at his home. That's why the book of Psalms says wisdom without deeds is like a large tree with shallow roots. It does not last. Without hospitality, happiness eludes us.

When I was teaching this part of the prayer to my congregation, I came across an extraordinary Jewish folktale. No one knows exactly who first told this story, but it was written down in the early twentieth century by a Yiddish novelist named I. L. Peretz. It tells of a rabbi from the Ukrainian town of Nemirov. During the most sacred week of the year—the days between Rosh Hashanah and Yom Kippur—this rabbi was always absent during the morning prayers. The people of the town were confused, but then they reasoned that he was up in heaven, conferring with God, at such a holy time.

One man, let's call him the skeptic, was not convinced. He decided to follow the rabbi. So early one morning he entered the rabbi's house and hid under the bed. He watched with surprise as the rabbi awoke, dressed in ragged clothes, and wrapped a leather belt around his waist. Then the rabbi grabbed an ax and set out for the forest. The skeptic quietly followed.

In the forest the rabbi chopped down a tree, tied up the wood with the rope he carried, and walked back into town. He then knocked on the door of a tiny shack. Inside was a very old woman, gnarled and ill. The rabbi introduced himself as a peasant named Vassily who had brought some wood for her fire. He entered, lit a fire, made tea, and talked with the woman. The skeptic watched all this through a crack in the door. Soon they both returned home, and the skeptic never breathed a word about what had happened that day. But every year, when the rabbi disappeared during that sacred week and the people said he had gone to heaven, the former skeptic would shake his head and murmur, "Maybe even higher."

Hospitality is not only inviting our neighbors over for dinner. It is extending ourselves for the benefit of others. The rabbi could not invite the homebound woman to his home. So he went to hers. He gave her his time and resources. This rabbi exemplified what the book of Genesis teaches in that famous question Cain poses to God, "Am I my brother's keeper?" Hospitality means answering that question with a yes.

The Hebrew word for "keeper" (as in "brother's keeper") is *shomer*. The word also means "guardian." We are one another's guardians through the ravages of life. That word, *guardian*, conveys the depth of the meaning of hospitality. Hospitality is not simply being nice. It is not simply meeting people's needs. In fact, I hesitated in using the word *hospitality* for this chapter because the word sometimes seems too corporate and bland. We have a "hospitality industry" and titles like "hospitality manager."

Real hospitality is a sacred commitment. We show it because God asks us to, not simply because we have good manners or we get paid for it. The Hebrew words with which we convey hospitality reflect that purpose. The words themselves convey a sacred energy.

Consider, for example, the traditional Jewish words of greeting. One of them is *shalom*. If we see someone we have not seen in a while, we say, "Shalom, *chaver*," which means "Welcome, friend." But it means more than that. *Shalom* doesn't only mean "hello" and "welcome." It means "peace, integrity, wholeness." When we say "Shalom, friend," we are saying to a friend or guest, "Your arrival makes me whole. You bring peace to this moment, to this place. You are meant to be here in this place at this time." The word *shalom* creates an instant connection.

Another traditional Hebrew greeting is *Baruch haBah*. The phrase means "Blessed are those who come." When we greet others with these words, we offer them a blessing. And we acknowledge that we are blessed by their arrival.

The Hebrew word *baruch*, "blessed," is a powerful one. It is related to the Hebrew word *berachim*, which means "knees." In ancient times a blessing was accompanied by the bending of the knees. Even today, some people greet one another with a short bow, a bending of the body. This act conveys respect. So does welcoming someone with a blessing.

Now, greeting others with words of blessing does not

guarantee happiness for the blesser or the blessed. Sometimes politeness is a veil for deception. But the words we use with one another—especially the guest and the stranger—make a difference. As I mentioned at the opening of this chapter, I first saw the sacred power of hospitality at the dinner table of my teacher and mentor, Professor Arnie Eisen. One act of blessing he did with his children has stayed with me and inspired me to do the same with my own. The first time I ever witnessed it was at his home.

At the dinner table, in front of friends and guests, he laid his hands on his son and invoked the traditional Jewish blessing on him. The customary blessing for boys includes the hope that they be "like Ephraim and Menasha." Ephraim and Menasha were the two sons of Joseph, the Hebrew boy who rose to become the vizier of Egypt in the book of Genesis. Before he died, Joseph's father Jacob gave the two brothers a special blessing. Aside from this appearance, however, the two brothers do not play major roles in the Biblical narrative.

Why, then, did the Jewish sages choose to use them as the role models for young boys? Surely they could have chosen more consequential figures: Abraham, Isaac, Jacob, or even Moses. They did so because Ephraim and Menasha were the first brothers in the Bible to get along with one another. Every prior set of siblings fails to do so. Cain kills Abel, Isaac has little contact with Ishmael, Jacob steals the birthright from Esau, and Joseph is sold into slavery by his brothers. After so many generations of conflict, we finally encounter a pair of brothers who do not harm one another.

By selecting Ephraim and Menasha, the sages sought to teach a lesson. Happiness begins with peace in the home. It begins with the blessings we give to one another.

Be There When Others Need You
ביקור חולים

"The door to happiness opens outward."
—Søren Kierkegaard

There is one moving prayer in Judaism that always makes me cry. It is called the Misheberach. It is a prayer for healing. Its words are simple: "May the source of strength, Who blessed the ones before us, help us find the courage to make our lives a blessing, and let us say, Amen. Bless those in need of healing with *r'fuah sh'leimah*, the renewal of body, the renewal of spirit, and let us say, Amen."

It's not the words of the prayer that spark tears as much as it is the melody. It builds up from short staccato notes to a deeper, heartfelt proclamation of hope. Some people tell me they come to worship just to hear that prayer.

While I cannot prove it, I suspect that the power of the prayer comes from more than the words and the melody. It comes from thinking about and picturing friends and family who are ill. The illness may be physical, mental, or spiritual. Our saying the prayer does not change their condition. It does not automatically heal them. But it changes our perspective. *It reminds us that who we are is shaped by those we care most about.*

It also leads us to look more closely at ourselves. When

saying the prayer, for example, I find myself feeling more grateful for my health, and more mindful of the well-being of my family and congregants. I think about the people I have encountered over the past week and the struggles they are undergoing.

The prayer also brings each of us face to face with our mortality. That is a gift. Unless we work in the health-care industry, most of us rarely encounter the ill and dying. They stay confined to hospitals or nursing homes. Other people wash and dress them. Many view the elderly as burdens to be set aside for others. But when we think and live this way, we lose perspective. We forget that death is a natural part of life. It happens to each of us.

Reverend Forrest Church illustrates this truth in a powerful example from his own upbringing. "I didn't live with death, but it was a constant visitor to my home," he writes. His maternal great-grandfather, Alexander Burnett, "and his enormous oxygen tank moved into my grandparents' home, where he took up residence on the living room couch. Every day he grew weaker and, if at all possible, quieter, and then, one sunny afternoon, passed away surrounded by family. The musty tang of his death is as vivid to me today as the smell of morning coffee. It was the most natural thing in the world."

When we distance ourselves from the sick and dying, we think we are protecting ourselves. But the truth is that we are producing unconscious guilt and sabotaging our pursuit of happiness. In this chapter we will learn how to become more mindful and committed to a different approach.

Why We Avoid Doing Something Good

None of us want to admit that we avoid visiting the ill and dying, but personal experiences tell me it is true. I have visited hundreds of people in the hospital who tell me I am the first person to visit them aside from their spouse and children. Families who have just lost a loved one often tell me hundreds of people wrote them to offer condolences, but few of them called or visited when their loved one was sick.

I gently tell the families that the lack of visits does not reflect a lack of concern. It simply reflects the unconscious fear many of us have when it comes to illness. And sometimes we do not know what to say. Should we talk about all the medical issues? That is rarely uplifting or helpful. Should we stick to simple platitudes? That seems inappropriate in a hospital, where life and death surround us. Here's what I tell myself: presence is what matters most. I once heard it said that 80 percent of life is showing up. When it comes to comforting the sick, it is 99 percent.

That's why the Jewish sages included it among our ten wisdom practices. And that's why they used the words they did. The critical word in the phrase *bikur cholim* is *bikur*. *Cholim* simply means "sick." *Bikur*, however, has multiple meanings, each of which adds a dimension to the phrase. These meanings illuminate the way we can find the greatest happiness and contribute the most value to the healing of the sick.

The first meaning is "to visit." An act of *bikur* involves physical presence. A call or e-mail does not hurt, but it is only a start. According to the Jewish sages, a personal visit changes us, and it encourages us to pray more for a person's healing. Our physical presence also creates bonds a virtual visit does not. Consider what psychologists now know about body language and physical connections. Looking a person directly in the eyes conveys interest. Physical touch—if permitted by the doctors—conveys caring. It reduces anxiety and puts a patient at ease. Physical touch can help even if it comes from a stranger. While the touch does not have direct medical effects—it cannot cure a cold or eliminate cancer cells—the reduction in stress it engenders can boost our immune system. We can heal more quickly. In other words, ancient healing practices have a basis in science. But we cannot overstay our welcome. We are not to overtax the sociability of the patient. My experience suggests that we should not stay longer than fifteen minutes.

The second meaning of *bikur* is "to discern." When we visit the sick, we are to discern their unique needs. We are to differentiate their needs from those of others. Then we try to meet those needs. If we discern they need a laugh, we can tell a joke. If they need to speak, we can listen. During one visit I made recently, the patient spent fifteen minutes lambasting the doctor's treatment. I came to learn from the family that the doctor was the best in his field and had been providing wonderful care. The man simply needed to vent. My presence offered him an opportunity to do so.

The need to vent is often a deeply felt one. My grandfather was a doctor for forty years, and he used to love to tell a joke about a certain type of patient. This patient—let's call him Goldberg—was at the famous Memorial Sloan Kettering Cancer Center in New York City. He was getting the finest treatment possible. Then, without warning, he checked himself out and checked into a run-down hospital miles away.

When the new doctor came into his room and looked at his chart, he asked him why he had transferred. "Was it the doctors?" he asked.

"The doctors? They were geniuses," Goldberg replied. "Wonderful. I can't complain."

"Was it the nurses?" the doctor continued.

"The nurses? Fantastic. Angels in human form, kind, attentive. About the nurses I can't complain."

"Was it the food?" the doctor asked incredulously.

"The food was divine. Like a world-class restaurant. About the food I can't complain."

The doctor looked frustrated. He asked Goldberg, "Why did you leave one of the greatest hospitals in the world and come here?"

Goldberg looked at him with a big smile. "Because here—here I can complain!"

Sometimes we can listen to a complaint, and everyone feels a little better.

The third meaning of *bikur* derives from its connection to another word—*boker*. *Boker* means "morning," as in the Hebrew phrase *Boker tov*, "Good morning." The morning is a time of brightness and hope, as in the phrase from the Bible, "Darkness may tarry through the night, but hope comes in the morning." Thus *bikur cholim* is an opportunity to bring hope and brightness to the sick. We have to be careful in doing so. Suggesting to a terminally ill person that they will get better does not lift anyone's spirits. It only makes our words seem superficial. Yet those who are sick often have a narrow perspective. The illness can feel so overwhelming that they do not see a way out. It is like getting stuck in a long dark tunnel. We do not see the light at its end. One of our tasks in visiting the sick is to show that light. We give hope and paint a picture of a different tomorrow.

I have found this task immensely fulfilling. A hospital or nursing home can feel dreary. Aside from children's hospitals, which offer a refreshing brightness and playfulness, many hospitals feel dark. A hopeful visit can change the patient's experience. And the shift in perspective can bring a fuller and quicker healing.

Why Visiting the Sick Provides the Visitor with a Healing Balm

Visiting the sick clearly makes the patient happier. But what can it do for us? What do we gain by taking time to visit, uplift, and meet another person's needs? We gain a deeper connection and greater comfort with our own vulnerabilities. And much more.

I have never visited someone in the hospital and then regretted doing so. A visit to someone in need always helps. Unless they request no visitors, someone who is ill benefits from not feeling isolated. And we see the uplift right away. We see what a difference our actions make. In other areas of life, we do not see the consequences of positive action. Think of investing, for example. We put money away for retirement. We pay taxes for social security. We may see small gains and losses over the years. But it is only when we start to use the money that we see the wisdom of our actions. But an act of *bikur cholim* yields immediate benefits. It does not require much time, intelligence, or money, but it gives us a feeling of accomplishment. We can do something to help somebody.

The benefits of visiting the sick can continue long after the visit itself. A rabbinic mentor once told me the story of a man who had a fatal illness and was in the hospital. After he had been there about a week, the man's wife called the rabbi, and told him that the man's best friend had not visited him in the hospital. It was not a matter of distance—the man's best friend was a physician in that hospital!

The rabbi called the physician and asked him why he hadn't

visited his best friend. The physician said he was terrified. He knew his friend's illness was fatal, and he also knew that he would break down and cry were he to visit. His tears, he said, would only make his friend more despondent and would not bring him any comfort or hope.

The rabbi persuaded him to go, telling him that it was okay to break down. His friend needed him. After making the initial visit, the man visited with his best friend every day, sometimes twice a day, until he died. He later thanked the rabbi for urging him to go, telling him that he could not have lived with himself had he not overcome his fear.

The lesson is clear. Visiting the sick does not only bring comfort to the patient. It also deepens our relationships. The sense of concern and hope expressed in a visit is impossible to convey in any other way.

This story not only moved me, it guided me. I was impressed by my mentor's willingness to give clear and direct instructions to the doctor. He told him he must go and visit his friend. In my earlier years as a rabbi, I probably would have said, "It would be a good idea to visit your friend. You've got to do what's best for you, but visiting might be really worthwhile." In other words, I would have been too vague. I would have lacked clarity and conviction because I thought my role was simply to listen, love, and empathize. But sometimes that's not enough. Sometimes we need to care enough to tell others what we truly believe.

Indeed, in living this practice of the happiness prayer, I saw that true caring involves doing and saying things that can feel uncomfortable. Sometimes ambivalence is a way of protecting ourselves. But faith means having the courage of our convictions.

Can I Pray for You?

One thing we can do for the sick—whether we visit personally or not—is pray for them. To my Christian readers, this language seems natural. For my Jewish and nonreligious readers, it probably sounds awkward. I confess it sounded that way to me the first time someone said to me, "I'm praying for you." It was during a summer I spent working as a chaplain at a hospital in New York City. I was part of a group of clergy in training—including a Carmelite priest, a nun, and a nondenominational evangelical pastor—all of whom were undergoing training in pastoral ministry. We combined visiting patients with group meetings in which we shared personal spiritual practices and exposed some of our vulnerabilities as clergy in training. It was a transformative—if sometimes disturbing and difficult—summer.

One of the participants always ended his time for speaking during the group sessions by saying, "I'm praying for you." And then he would say it to each of us personally. I asked him after a session what he was praying for. He said, "For you to know the truth." My immediate feeling was anger. Was he seeking to convert me? Did his words violate the spirit of respect we sought to maintain in this multifaith program?

Rather than confront him, I asked him to sit down for coffee. We talked, and he told me how deeply he believed in the power of prayer. God hears its words. His prayer was not for me to convert. His prayer was for God to grant me grace. Whether or not I shared his understanding of grace was immaterial. It was a way of caring.

Not only did his words feel genuine, he was the most successful of all of the student chaplains. Patients reported to our supervisor that his visits lifted their spirits and made them feel more comfortable and hopeful. We all asked him what his secret was. He said simply, "I pray for my patients." His prayer involved more than words. It brought faith, hope, and empathy. The patients knew he cared for them. The patients knew he meant what he said. He was not going through the motions. He was praying from his heart.

That's the power of prayer. Its words are what Rabbi Lawrence Kushner calls "invisible lines of connection." They draw us close to God and to one another. And they can heal.

A recent study, for example, at San Francisco General Hospital examined the effect of prayer on 393 cardiac patients. Half of them were prayed for by strangers who had only the patients' names, and the other half were not. The patients who knew people were praying for them had fewer complications and cases of pneumonia, and they needed less drug treatment. They also got better faster and left the hospital earlier.

The difference between these patients and the others was not medical treatment. They all had the same doctors and nurses. It was the knowledge that they were not alone. Others were praying for them.

When others pray for us, we also become more comfortable with praying and saying aloud our own pains, feelings, and desires. I once visited a member of my congregation at the hospital. When I walked in the door, his first words to me were, "Rabbi, my wife wanted you to come see me. But I have to tell you I don't believe in God. Why would I have pancreatic cancer if there is a God?"

Talk about cutting right to the chase.

We talked for a while over several visits, and while we didn't solve all his theological concerns, we got to a feeling of comfort and acceptance. He still insisted there was no God, but he didn't mind my praying for him. In fact, he said to me once as I was leaving, "Keep saying those prayers for me."

After he passed away, I met with members of the family to discuss his life and prepare for the funeral. Before I left, his wife pulled out a folder and handed it to me. "What is it?" I asked.

"It's the prayers Jack said while in the hospital. He said them aloud to himself every day." I looked down at a sheet and saw passages from the Bible and from several authors we had discussed. Among them was a prayer attributed to Reinhold Niebuhr: "God, grant me the serenity to accept the things I cannot change; the courage to change the things I can; and the wisdom to know the difference." Shocked, I asked his wife when he had started saying these prayers. "After your visits," she said. "And it brought him so much comfort." I do not know whether he believed the words he said or not. But they worked. They brought him a sense of peace that eluded him elsewhere. It all began with a relationship triggered by a visit to the hospital.

That experience reminds us of what happiness is and is not. Happiness is not always pleasure. It is not always ease. It is connection. It is a recognition that life's fragilities present us with opportunities for meaning.

In another hospital visit, I met with a husband and his wife, who had just undergone major surgery. She was in a dazed and confused state. Still, I put my hand on her shoulder and began saying the words of the Shema, the most well-known Jewish prayer. As I began the second verse, she opened her eyes, moved her lips, and said the words in a soft voice. When we finished, she went right into a deep sleep. I looked at the husband with surprise. He wore a look of shock. We didn't talk about it, though, and I said my goodbyes and promised to visit again the next week. I did, and soon she returned home in good health.

About four months later, right before the major Jewish holidays, I got an e-mail from the couple. It said, "Rabbi, I find it hard to describe the impact of that first visit on our lives. We didn't know if Jackie was going to make it. After that prayer, we somehow knew she would. Our life has changed dramatically. We express our love for each other more. We take less for granted. Every day is a gift."

These were not just words. I saw it in the way they lived. Sometimes God gives us a glimpse of the meaning and purpose of life. That is a precious gift, and when we visit others in need, we can become the bearer of it. Even though I make lots of hospital visits, moments like these remind me of the true path to happiness.

How Do We Heal?

The study I cited above about the patients at San Francisco General Hospital was almost anonymous. The people saying the prayers knew only the names of those for whom they were praying. They did not know anything else about them. And the patients still healed more quickly. When prayers emerge from a real relationship, they likely exert even more influence on the patient.

Now, no study has looked at the difference between praying for people we know and praying for people we do not know. Jewish wisdom, however, suggests *the relationship contributes to healing*. In other words, our connection to the person who is visiting and praying for us brings another dimension to our healing.

I first learned this truth in an enigmatic story from the Jewish sages. It tells of a time when a famous rabbi named Yochanan got sick. His colleague Rabbi Hanina went to visit. Hanina posed a question to his friend: "Are your sufferings cherished by you?" Yochanan replied, "Neither they nor their reward." Then Hanina said, "Give me your hand." Yochanan gave him his hand, and Hanina raised him up from his sickbed.

The incident poses several questions. Was it a miraculous healing? If so, couldn't Yochanan simply have drawn from the same power to heal himself? In response to these implicit questions, the Talmud answers, "A prisoner cannot free himself." In other words, a patient cannot heal himself. We need others. Those others serve as God's intermediaries. Even a rabbi as great as Yochanan needed another person. We need another's love and caring to heal.

The power of relationship in healing is something I learned from my father. As I mentioned in an earlier chapter, he is a psychiatrist. He talks with patients, and through those sessions forms a connection—known as the therapeutic relationship—that plays a critical role in healing. As he often tells me, he does not heal anyone. The relationship helps people heal themselves. We often talk about what his experiences can teach me and other clergy.

His early training denigrated the role of religion. While a proud Jew, Sigmund Freud, the founder of modern psychiatry, saw religion as a neurosis, an infantile yearning for a father figure. Part of maturing, he wrote, was moving beyond the religious illusion.

My father arrived at a different conclusion. His generation of therapists tended to be more open to the role of faith in their patients' lives. If a patient's faith could contribute to their healing, they nurtured it. One evening we were invited to present a discussion about faith and psychotherapy at his synagogue. I shared the story of Hanina and Yochanan, and we came to the conclusion that each had had faith in the relationship. It was not necessarily miraculous healing. Hanina did not have a magical touch that healed his friend. The healing came out of the relationship. The actual healing may not have even been physical. The text is not clear about whether Yochanan lived much longer. We do know, however, that he experienced a renewed well-being.

A Different Kind of Healing

In the Misheberach prayer with which we opened the chapter, we learned that healing is not always physical. It is often spiritual. A few years ago, I went to visit a longtime member of my synagogue. In his upper eighties, he had been in and out of the hospital for months. The end was near. The man had mixed relationships with his four children. No one was estranged from anyone else, but they had experienced differing levels of financial success and family stability. I had become personally close with one of them, who had been doing much of the day-to-day care for her dad.

When I arrived in the hospital room, they were having "the talk." This is the conversation about what happens after a parent dies. Ideally parents and children have this conversation long before the time comes. But many do not. The delay means they are forced to have a difficult conversation when they are stressed and concerned and short on sleep. These conversations often become hostile and painful, especially when other underlying issues remain.

The tension was palpable when I walked into the hospital room. One son was sweating and had an angry look on his face. The other had his head down in his hands. The daughter sat closest to their father, her hand on his shoulder. The other son was missing. The father seemed to get smaller in his hospital bed. He did not know how to address the tension between himself and the children, and among the four children themselves. Even if he had, his wife—who had died two years earlier—had been the one most concerned with how their children got along. Nothing I could say would resolve the all the financial and personal stresses in the room. Nothing I could say would make past go away.

What I could do was focus attention on the meaning of the moment. With the right words, I could help them attain something more important to their well-being than money. They could find a measure of understanding and healing. An impending death clarifies what is important, but not only for the person who is dying. It can do so with the people close to them. My task was to bring about this clarity.

I started by reframing the purpose of the conversation. I told the story of Moses and his siblings Miriam and Aaron. In the biblical book of Numbers, Miriam and Aaron gossip about Moses and his wife Zipporah. This gossip reflected their jealousy and hostility. God struck Miriam with leprosy as a punishment. Aaron was not punished directly, though he dies a few chapters later.

After Miriam was struck with leprosy, Moses was beside himself. He was not interested in punishing her for gossiping. He simply wanted to heal his sister. He uttered the first prayer of the Bible. It is only five words long (in Hebrew). In English it reads, "God, please heal her." Its brevity and directness suggest Moses spoke from the heart. His simple words were a plea to

God—a plea for God to remember that some things are more important than petty jealousies. Moses, Miriam, and Aaron were family, and they also had a mission to fulfill—to bring the Israelites to the Promised Land.

The four people sitting in the hospital room before me were family, and the three adult children shared much more than anger and jealousy. They shared a love of their dad and a desire to let him die in peace. I spoke a prayer invoking those emotions. It came from a feeling of empathy for their dad. I knew he loved his children, and from what I knew from the daughter, they loved him in spite of all their issues.

A great twelfth-century Jewish philosopher named Solomon ibn Gabriel said that words from the heart enter to the heart. The prayer I said came from the heart, and when it ended, a different feeling filled the room. The children began speaking with one another. Their father began to gesture and smile more. Healing had begun.

I did not stay for the financial discussion. But when it came time for me to conduct the funeral, I met with the children again, and they spoke with ease and affection. They spoke of their happy memories of their father. Even the brother who hadn't been there in the hospital room seemed to get along with his siblings.

A prayer of healing helps us shift perspective. It lets us see our lives from what philosopher Baruch Spinoza called "the point of view of eternity." And anyone can evoke that perspective. Even a kind word from a nurse or a doctor can help us heal, and bring us from self-pity to greater awareness. Just think about moments in your life when a kind word changed everything. Prayers of healing do that in unexpected ways. They change our perspective.

Changing Me

I did not always appreciate the power of healing prayer. That may seem strange coming from a rabbi. But prayer became essential in coping with my own struggles. At age thirty, when I encountered the enormous personal and spiritual challenges of leading a large congregation, I gravitated toward sources of guidance in my comfort zone. I talked to my dad. I talked to my mentors. I read books.

But it was the happiness prayer that got me through. Yet even before I discovered the happiness prayer, I began to appreciate the power of a healing prayer in a deeper way. It began right around the birth of my first child. A few days after that birth, as we were struggling with her health issues, I visited a couple in my synagogue who had just delivered premature twin girls. The twins were in the infant intensive care unit in the same hospital where my wife had just given birth. The girls stayed in that hospital for about two months.

I had married the couple a few years before. They'd wanted children so badly. Their gratitude for having been able to have children, even children born early, helped them get through the harrowing months in the hospital. Yet after they went home, problems persisted. One of the children needed open-heart surgery from a specialist in Boston. Complications arose after the surgery, and the infant died a month later.

After the funeral, more problems arose. The parents' jobs suffered, and so did the twin who'd survived. A year after their birth, the parents asked me to do a Hebrew naming ceremony for the surviving daughter. This is an adaptation of the traditional Jewish ceremony done for boys on the eighth day after birth, when they are circumcised and given a Hebrew name.

Girls often receive a Hebrew name in conjunction with their first birthday.

I tried to use my remarks and prayers at the naming to bring some healing and comfort to the parents. I recognized the sacrifices they had made and the courage with which they had dealt with uncertainty and loss. Their experiences, I said, reminded us all of the need to treasure the lives and responsibilities we have. After I said these words, I thought to myself that I was being too naive and light. Of course we needed to treasure life and live with purpose. But who was I to say such things in front of parents who had gone through so much?

Then the mother came up and gave an extraordinary speech. She said she and her family were lucky. They had seen what it meant not to take life for granted, and they had met families who'd lost far more than they had. She said she was lucky to have had their deceased daughter for the time she had. Then she said the words of Psalm 23. "Yea, though I walk through the valley of the shadow of death, I shall fear no evil, for You are with me."

When she said it, we all felt it. We all felt a deeper appreciation for life. Prayer is more than saying a few kind words. It is a way of affirming that life has meaning even through pain and loss. It is a way of affirming that healing is possible for anyone, anywhere.

Celebrate Good Times
הכנסת כלה

"Life is about loving and being loved. It is about enjoying your food and sitting in the sun rather than rushing through lunch and hurrying back to the office. It is about savoring the beauty of moments that don't last, the sunsets, the leaves turning color, the rare moments of true human communication."

—Rabbi Harold Kushner

The film and musical *Fiddler on the Roof* was one of the great surprise hits of the twentieth century. Telling the story of a Jewish village in eastern Europe at the turn of the nineteenth century, it was acclaimed throughout the world, even in Japan, which has virtually no Jewish residents. What made this story so powerful?

In part it was the cross-cultural theme of tensions between parents and children, the old ways and the new ways. Every culture faces these tensions. It also showcased a close-knit community that shared joys and deep sorrows together. That portrayal is the part most relevant to our pursuit of happiness. Its essence is captured in my favorite scene in the movie—the wedding of one of Reb Tevye's daughters.

Reb Tevye is the main character—a humble milkman trying to eke out a living and a decent life for his wife and five children. He is committed to putting on a perfect wedding for his oldest daughter. The bride appears dressed radiantly in white. But then the most wonderful thing happens. The town square fills with people. The entire town is present. That is because in Judaism a wedding is a community affair. It is not only for the bride and groom to celebrate. If that were the case, most weddings would take place in the rabbi's study. Rather, a wedding brings together a community to celebrate. The community witnesses and affirms the marriage between two individuals. Judaism teaches that it is a commandment, no less important than keeping the Sabbath or praying, to celebrate with the bride and groom.

This tradition may seem a bit anachronistic, especially in an era when more and more people are living single. But celebrating life's sacred moments—our own and those of others—is part of the recipe for a happy, fulfilling life. (The literal translation for this wisdom practice is "welcome the bride," and I am using the practice as an example of celebrating sacred moments.) Just as visiting the sick draws us into another person's pain, so dancing and singing and celebrating at a wedding draw us into another person's joy. More specifically, celebrating with a bride and groom draws us into communal joy. Sharing in another's celebration takes us deep into community.

Sometimes going deep can create discomfort. During the wedding scene in the film version of *Fiddler on the Roof*, the camera pans to the different people attending, including the man to whom Reb Tevye had once promised his daughter in marriage. His daughter did not like that man. So Tevye broke off the engagement, infuriating the would-be groom. Yet that spurned man still came to celebrate the wedding as a member of the community. That's what community does. It brings different people together.

At a Jewish wedding, the host is expected to invite rich and poor, friend and enemy, boss and secretary. And the host makes every effort to ensure that all feel welcome. That's why the bride and groom are required to wear only plain gold bands during the ceremony. Any more elaborate band would make poorer members of the community feel uncomfortable.

The burden, however, is not only on the host. He is supposed to invite everybody. And everyone is expected to come. Hence our wisdom practice: celebrate with bride and groom. Mark that sacred moment with them. We need one another to live a happier life.

When people lived in small villages, celebrating sacred moments with the entire community was easier. We simply had to ring the bell and assemble in the village square. Today it takes more work and expense. Yet I have seen people embrace this wisdom practice repeatedly and successfully. Think back to your twenties and thirties. When a friend or relative invited you to their wedding, did you make every effort to attend? Did you stretch your budget and maybe spend a little more than you should have to get to the wedding and give a gift?

My wife and I did. So have many of the couples I have married. The reason is not simply that weddings are fun. It is not simply that a wedding is a major life event. We usually don't make the same effort to travel cross-country for a friend's graduation. A wedding is about more than community. A wedding reminds us of something bigger than ourselves. It reminds us that life is fragile. And we need to embrace every opportunity to celebrate.

Why *Wedding Crashers* Was a Hit Movie

When we celebrate with bride and groom, some of their joy rubs off on us. I always suspected this was true. Yet new findings in the field of neuroscience prove it. Scientists have discovered what they call "mirror neurons." These are parts of the brain that lead us to mirror the emotions of the people around us. When they feel joy, so do we. This tendency to mirror emotions seems to be wired into our brains. Think about babies who smile and coo when you look at and laugh with them. They are mirroring our emotions.

The science behind the way this mirroring works is complex, and our understanding of it is ever evolving. Mirroring is not always automatic. Our own feelings at the time and our relationships with the people around us affect our response. Mirror neurons, however, are embedded within us. They have helped us survive as human beings by creating bonds among us.

Celebrating with a bride and groom triggers mirror neurons because we are directly witnessing others' joy. When they are triggered, we begin to think about performing similar actions. One scientist has written that with mirror neurons "we can instantly experience a situation or a person's feelings as if it is happening to us because these neurons pretend we are experiencing what we observe." I have married many couples who met one another at a mutual friend's wedding. Subconsciously or not, they may have pictured themselves getting married and sharing the emotions of their friends. That picture likely shaped their relationship.

Of course, many other factors could explain why a disproportionate number of people I have married met one another at a mutual friend's wedding. Yet mirror neurons would explain this phenomenon precisely. We witness the joy of a friend and begin to move toward experiencing it ourselves. Most weddings evoke a pervasive feeling of happiness. I sometimes tell couples that they are doing their friends and family a favor by inviting them to their wedding. They are giving their guests the opportunity to get a taste of the joy the bride and groom feel.

I suspect this truth was one reason for the success of the movie *Wedding Crashers*. That film features Owen Wilson and Vince Vaughn as friends who pretend to be guests at weddings. They meet women and get free food and drinks. Ultimately they have to reveal their real identities when they fall in love with people they meet. Even the crashers cannot resist the joy triggered by the wedding ceremonies. They ultimately become better people, with greater empathy and honesty. Such is the power of mirror neurons and the wisdom practice of celebrating with bride and groom.

It is not only at weddings that we participate and share in another's joy. The same experience can happen at a big birthday party, a retirement celebration, an anniversary, or a baby naming. What these occasions share is that they brim with emotional power. Experiencing these emotions changes us.

To understand how, ask yourself a simple question: Why do people cry at weddings? We know why we cry at funerals. We feel loss and will never see that person on earth again. A wedding, however, is a time of joy. Why do we cry? Because we are becoming different people. If we are friends of the bride, we now have to relate to her as a part of a married couple. If we are parents of the groom, we have new members of our family whom we may not have chosen, but who have become part of us nonetheless. If we are celebrating another friend's birthday, we realize we are getting older.

108

Returning to *Fiddler on the Roof*, we see this truth captured in a verse of one of its signature songs, "Sunrise, Sunset." Looking at their daughter, the parents of the bride ask, "Where is the little girl I carried? Where is the little boy at play? I don't remember getting older; when did they?" These celebrations create liminal moments, pushing us to look at our lives from a broader perspective. We recall our losses and gains, where we erred and where we succeeded. We recognize our humanity— that we are not the same people we once were and that we will continue to change in the years ahead.

Recognizing those changes unsettles us at first. That's one of the reasons brides and grooms often get nervous at a wedding. I've seen it dozens of times. Change is a form of loss. Meaningful changes lead to the loss of some of the patterns of life that made us who we are. Even when we have prepared for a change and understand the reason behind it, we often resist it. I've known moms and dads, for example, who are very excited about the birth of a child. Yet just as the baby is about to be born, they express great fear, and wonder whether they are ready for this tremendous change. Of course, in every case they have gone on to have the child and adapted to this new reality with joy. They have overcome their resistance. And that creates joy.

Such liminal experiences also clarify our values because struggle and change are not only about loss. They are about affirmation. In his book *The Practice of Adaptive Leadership: Tools and Tactics for Changing Your Organization*, Harvard professor Ronald Heifetz addresses this phenomenon and points out that an experience of change can be an opportunity to remember the foundations on which we built that change. We ask ourselves, "Of all that we care about, what elements are essential and must be preserved into the future, or we will lose who we are?" Change is a chance to remind ourselves of the unique characteristics that make us who we are.

In the context of marriage, celebrating with bride and groom can help us see what really sustains our friendships. When we see a friend describe what he loves in his wife, we see what really matters to him, and the way in which similar qualities or values matter to us. On the other hand, have you ever been to a person's wedding and then not really kept in touch with them in the years following? I can think of half a dozen people at my wedding whom I have barely spoken to since that time. Nothing dramatic happened. We simply drifted apart. That may seem like a loss. But we can also see it as a gain. We have gained clarity about who we are and what we value.

At liminal moments like a wedding, we see life with a clarity that otherwise eludes us. The people and principles that matter most become clearer, and we can resolve to focus our lives on what we know is important. As a rabbi I get to experience these moments frequently, and that is the greatest benefit of my work. I am constantly reminded of what matters most. This clarity helps me get through the drudgery we all face in life. It lets me ignore the constant advertisements promising higher status with this car, greater wealth with this investment strategy, and a better body with this diet. Such distractions keep us away from the practices—taught in the happiness prayer—that bring true well-being.

Love, Happiness, and Revenge

A wedding brings together two individuals. It also unites two families and the communities of which they are a part. Before the wedding ceremony, the families and couple join together in a ritual known as the signing of the *ketubah*. A *ketubah* is a symbolic Jewish marriage contract. It is a written document expressing the couple's commitment to one another. The words are frequently surrounded by art. The *ketubah* has no legal significance except in a small segment of the Orthodox Jewish community. Rather, it serves as a visual symbol of marital vows.

When I lead a *ketubah*-signing ceremony, I always invite the living parents and grandparents of the bride and groom to take hold of the ketubah and give it to the couple. They are passing on their experience of commitment and love. As they do so, I recount the names of family members who have died. I describe the ways they helped shape the bride and groom and their families. That moment is always among the most moving and memorable of the wedding ceremony. Tears usually form in parents' eyes.

Then friends of the couple sign the *ketubah*. The signers cannot be blood relatives. This custom reinforces the idea that a wedding is not only for the bride and groom. Their joy echoes in their community of friends and family. The Jewish sages even describe signing a *ketubah* as a *simcha*, a happy occasion, for the friends who sign it.

That's a special kind of happiness. It's opposite of schadenfreude, enjoyment of another's pain. Here we enjoy another's happiness. Unfortunately, the English language does not have a word to capture that feeling. Yiddish, however, does. Yiddish is a language combining Hebrew and German. It was spoken by many Jewish communities in eastern Europe during the eighteenth, nineteenth, and early twentieth centuries. Some immigrants in the United States continued to speak it into the 1980s, but it has slowly diminished as a living language. A few of its words, however, have entered into English: words like *shlep*, *mensch*, and *shtick*.

One Yiddish word used frequently in the Jewish community is *naches*. *Naches* is joy derived from the happiness of another person. Parents often use it to express pride in their children. A mom might say she gets *naches* from her daughter's success. But the term has wider meaning. We can get *naches* from a friend or a member of our community we do not know well. Someone who signs a *ketubah* gets *naches* from the experience. Someone who attends a wedding or even reads about it on Facebook can get *naches* from it. One of the most common forms of *naches* is the kind a teacher gets from students.

When I became the lead rabbi at Congregation Solel, a high school teacher sent me a note describing the *naches* he felt. As I struggled to become a better leader, I pictured the feeling of *naches* I hoped to evoke in the congregation. I wanted them to take pride in their rabbi, in knowing their spiritual leader could guide and comfort them. And I wanted them to give me *naches* by living sacred and just lives. Our potential for *naches* is limited only by the number of people in the world. We can find it wherever we are.

As a rabbi, I am fortunate to get *naches* from the couples I marry, students I bar and bat mitzvah, and babies I bless. These opportunities may be why clergy tend to be among the happiest professionals. But such opportunities are not limited to clergy. Attending a house of worship regularly exposes us to baptisms, communions, and other coming-of-age ceremonies. Participating in a community gives us opportunities to celebrate with others. In other words, we get *naches* when we look for and seek it out.

Almost any occasion provides an opportunity for *naches*. Hallmark has taken advantage of this truth and created an entire industry around it. Nothing in the Bible or any other sacred text, for example, talks about anniversaries. We do not know if our ancestors even noted the date of a marriage. But marking anniversaries today is almost mandatory for couples. But this type of commemoration does not only bring *naches*. It can change our lives and perspective.

One couple with whom I became quite close in the synagogue reached their seventieth anniversary. (They actually made it to seventy-five, and shortly afterward the husband passed away at age ninety-seven.) Few people have seventy years of experience as a couple. I wanted to honor the couple and find a way for the community to benefit from their wisdom. I asked them to deliver a joint sermon on the Friday night of their anniversary.

They spoke, and among the most moving of their remarks concerned their losing an adult child to cancer. When this happened they'd felt God had violated the natural order. Children are supposed to bury their parents, not vice versa. Their anger and sadness hurt their marriage. They fought over little issues. Then they did something grounded in faith. They went back to their vows and realized they'd made those vows for moments like these. Now they would really discover what it meant to be there for each other through life and death.

It was an extraordinary moment. Without that sermon the congregation would not have had the opportunity to hear and find inspiration from them. I got a little nervous during their speech because many members of the community had gone through divorces. And many were single and looking for a relationship. I feared this celebration of a marriage might make them feel out of place or like second-class citizens. In fact, the entire focus in this wisdom practice on marriage initially made me feel uncomfortable. While marriage is a gift for some, it is also something that does not work out for many.

Beforehand I'd shared some of my fears with divorced and

single members of my congregation, and they'd told me such celebrations and affirmations of marriage did not alienate them. In fact, they made them feel grateful to know such joy was possible. The one thing they asked me to do was recognize and honor the truth that marriage is often difficult and complex. Every couple goes through different experiences, and those experiences can break some relationships. Real community does not mean everyone does the same thing. It means we share one another's joy and feel one another's pain.

The real power of rituals is that they give us a framework with which to make sense of the experiences of life. They give us an opportunity to share those experiences with others. They brim with meaning and influence. Most importantly, they shape what we pay attention to. They honor what we value and care about. A ritual around graduation reflects our commitment to education. A ritual around naming a child reflects our commitment to the next generation. Rituals and values go hand in hand.

An ethical life without ritual is like a rose plucked from the soil. It may live, as one rabbi put it, for a while, but it will not sustain itself. Ideas need concrete expressions. Rituals add meaning to life by translating big ideas and felt human needs into concrete practices and tangible forms of support.

By adding meaning to our lives, rituals make us happier. This happiness can be both immediate and long lasting. Consider this clever study designed by Professor Heidi Halvorson. She invited an equal number of men and women to eat a chocolate bar. (She probably did not have a hard time recruiting participants.) She instructed some to eat the bar with a particular ritual. They would break the bar in half without unwrapping it, then unwrap half the bar and eat it, and then unwrap the other half and eat it. The other group would eat the bar as they normally would.

The group who ate with the ritual reported "finding the chocolate more flavorful and enjoying it more. They also took more time to savor it, and were willing to pay nearly twice as much for more of it." Rituals can make the ordinary feel extraordinary.

Inviting Us to Joy

Part of a ritual's power is the way it invites us in. But there's a problem with religious rituals. The traditional Jewish wedding ceremony, for example, is male centered. Its focal point is the groom giving the bride a ring and pronouncing her his wife. The bride has to accept the ring in front of two witnesses, yet the obligation to initiate the act and give a ring is solely the groom's. His words create the marriage. The bride simply accepts what is given to her. Her role in a traditional Jewish wedding ceremony is secondary.

Many women find that the traditional ring ceremony does not invite them in. It feels demeaning and antiquated. When all the power rests in the groom, both the couple and guests can also feel excluded and alienated. Instead of uplifting and deepening an experience of celebrating a relationship, the ritual can undermine it. I've talked to some couples who decided to get a civil marriage license at a courthouse rather than experience a traditional ceremony because they saw it as demeaning and alienating.

When women began to publicly express that feeling in the 1960s and 1970s, rabbis adapted the ritual. They inserted language instructing the bride to give the groom a ring as well. This "double ring" ceremony has become the standard in most

Jewish ceremonies around the world. We celebrate with bride and groom in a way that invites us in rather than pushes us out.

Their flexibility makes rituals a way of balancing the past and the present. They root us in tradition but speak to us where we are. That's part of what makes them so powerful and lasting. We can compare adapting rituals to adapting language. The English of Shakespeare is not identical to the English of today. But it is still the same language. Similarly, even as we adapt its details, the wedding ceremony of today echoes the one performed two thousand years ago. Both lift human acts into a divine orbit.

The variety of possible rituals is astounding. One woman I know asked me for a ritual for cleaning out her parents' home after they passed away. A particularly joyful ritual is the naming of a baby. In Jewish tradition a child is typically given a Hebrew name at eight days old. That name is used at Jewish life events, like the Bar or Bat Mitzvah ceremony, weddings, and funerals. Frequently parents choose a name to remind them of a loved one who has recently died. A name brings that person's spirit to life. A name can also represent an aspiration to certain character traits. My oldest daughter is named Hannah. We chose the name because she was born shortly after my grandmother Harriett died. But Hannah also means "kind" in Hebrew. We pray that she embodies kindness.

One of the reasons we follow a ritual in giving a Hebrew name is that a name is more than a personal identifier. It encompasses how we see and present ourselves in the world. Two thousand years ago the Jewish sages taught that we have three names. We have the name our parents give us, the name our friends call us, and the name we earn for ourselves in the world. Our task is to make them one. Fulfilling this task not only makes us happier, it also brings fulfillment and satisfaction.

One member of my synagogue who is an accomplished public servant and civic leader in Chicago used to tell a version of this truth to his coworkers. "We each have three names," he said. "The name we call ourselves. The name others call us. And the name we think others call us." Happiness comes from making sure they are all the same name.

Writing Your Life Story

Achieving that unity is a lifelong journey. Rituals like birthdays and weddings are part of that journey. They help us create our life story. At times that story can seem random. A marriage can break up, and we wonder how our life became such a mess. But then we meet someone who brings joy to our life in unimagined ways. We fail to get the job we want, but then end up in the job we love. Our children do not become the people we hoped they would be. But they become who they were meant to be.

Not everything turns out as we expect. Not everything ties up neatly together. But rituals help us discern a unity. They help connect the dots and put the pieces back together.

There is another Yiddish word that captures this truth. It is *besheret*. The closest English translation is "meant to be." The word *besheret* is usually used in romantic context. A person is another's *besheret*, their life partner, the person with whom they were meant to spend the rest of their life. But its true Yiddish meaning is about more than relationships. It is the belief that everything happens for a reason.

We cannot prove this truth. And sometimes people abuse it. They say someone who is suffering from an awful illness must have done something to deserve it. That is not the meaning of *besheret*. Rather, *besheret* is seeing an underlying pattern in our lives. It is looking back and seeing the contours of a story we did not see in the moment.

A friend, Rabbi Jonathan Miller, captured the idea of *besheret* beautifully when he spoke at a major ritual—his son's ordination as a rabbi. Jonathan is a rabbi in Birmingham, Alabama, but grew up on the East Coast. His entire family is there. His father and grandfather were rabbis there. When he was called to Birmingham, he barely knew where it was. The world's image of Birmingham at the time was primarily that of Commissioner of Public Safety Bull Connor, who used powerful hoses on African American civil rights marchers. When he arrived in Birmingham, Rabbi Miller said, he was "a stranger in a strange land."

But then *besheret* happened. He has remained at the synagogue in Birmingham for his entire career. Most rabbis move to a bigger congregation a few times in their career. But he grew as the city grew. He changed as it changed. Sure, someone could conclude that that was just luck. Birmingham was the right place at the right time for the right person. That's one perspective. That's the same perspective that sees the moments of our lives as random and unconnected. But there is another explanation: our stories unfold in the way they are meant to.

As Rabbi Miller's wife Judi put it at the ordination ceremony for their son, "We, the Miller family, were not planning on spending our lives in Birmingham, Alabama, when we arrived as 'strangers in a strange land.' Over the course of Jonathan's career, other congregations called him to come, but God called us to stay with you. Aaron told me that he decided to be a rabbi as he grew up among you and witnessed the meaning and value of his dad's calling. Had you been a less kind congregation, had there been fewer angels among you, his eyes may not have been opened in that way. Each one of you has, in some way, shepherded Aaron to his calling. And so I thank you, and God thanks you, for raising our child to serve our Jewish people."

Judi's words reveal not only the meaning of *besheret*, but also the power of ritual to draw meaning out of our sacred moments. Without the ritual of ordination, her words about God's role in keeping their family in Birmingham and nurturing their son to the clergy would likely have remained inside. They would not have provided a moment for a community to celebrate and understand its significance in nurturing a family.

Ritual puts us in a living relationship with the past, present, and future. Their son Aaron was becoming a rabbi that day. But that day was also part of a story that began before he was born and will continue after he is gone. The lives he will shape as a rabbi—the joys he will celebrate and create for others—are connected to the experiences of that community in Birmingham. The ritual of ordination brought them all together. So can the rituals we bring into our own lives.

We are part of a story that began before us and will continue after us. Picture your life as a book. When you celebrate sacred moments in your life, you fill the pages of that book with words of joy. When you share in the sacred moments of others, you add color and illustrations to those words. Your story brims with meaning and happiness, and your cup, as the Bible puts it, overflows.

Support Yourself and Others during Times of Loss

לוית המת

"He who should teach men to die would at the same time teach them to live."

—Michel de Montaigne

If you attend a Jewish worship service on Friday night or Saturday morning, you will encounter a unique custom. Near the end of the service, the rabbi retrieves a list of names and reads them to the assembled community. Occasionally someone will rise from their seat as a name is read. As soon as the entire list is read, everyone in the sanctuary stands up and joins together in a prayer.

The prayer is written in a combination of Hebrew and Aramaic, a historic language spoken for six hundred years in the ancient Near East. It has been recited in Jewish worship for about two thousand years. The words praise God and acknowledge God's kingship over the world. While they do not mention death or dying, they have become our primary prayer for solace and memory. The Kaddish, as the prayer is called, is the Jewish prayer of mourning.

The people who stand up first are observing a *yahrzeit*. A *yahrzeit* is the anniversary of a loved one's death. Reciting the words of the Kaddish prayer honors and helps us remember those loved ones. To observe a *yahrzeit* is one of the main reasons people come to Jewish worship services. As many have told me, they see marking a *yahrzeit* as a responsibility to their ancestors. The pull of the past—of memory—is strong. This is true not only in Judaism. Just visit a Catholic church and see the candles lit in memory and love.

But the Jewish way of remembering and mourning has a unique teaching. I had always taken it for granted, but I realized how peculiar it was when I spoke to a confirmation class from a neighboring church. This class had attended a service and stayed for a question-and-answer session. One student asked a question about the Kaddish prayer. "Why did you read all the names?" she asked. "To remember them because they died at this time years ago," I responded. "And what is the prayer about?" she continued. "It's about thanking God for their lives," I answered.

These were all standard questions I had heard many times. Then she asked, "Why do you remember the day a person died? Why not a person's birthday?"

This simple question had never occurred to me. I realized then that this Jewish practice is peculiar. Think about American culture. We celebrate George Washington's *birthday*. We remember Lincoln's *birthday*. Martin Luther King Day is the anniversary of his birth. Why do Jews remember the day of a person's death?

We will unpack some of the reasons in this chapter. The most basic answer is that *we can make sense of a life only when we look at it as a whole*. A birthday represents potential. We do not know who a baby will become. When a loved one dies, however, we can look at their life as a whole. We can make sense of the entire journey.

A story from the Talmud elaborates on the wisdom behind our practice. A man is sitting by a harbor, watching the ships come and go. A crowd of people is nearby. Everyone is cheering an outgoing ship, giving it a hearty send-off. But the incoming ships are scarcely noticed.

This wise man chastises the people's reactions. "Rejoice not," he says, "over the ship that is setting out to sea. For you know not what destiny awaits it, what storms it may encounter, what dangers lurk before it. Rejoice rather over the ship that has reached port safely and brought back all its passengers in peace."

It is the way of the world that when a human being is born, everyone rejoices. When a loved one dies, all feel sorrow. But we can also struggle to see it the opposite way. Nobody knows what troubles await the developing child on its journey through life. But when a person has lived all their days, we can take comfort in the knowledge that they have completed their journey successfully.

That's one of the truths we learn when we follow the wisdom practice of *levayat hamet*. The Hebrew words mean "accompany the dead." That word *accompany* refers literally to our responsibility to walk with the casket to its resting place. But it means much more. Its broader meaning is captured in the Hebrew phrase *nihum avelim*, which means "comforting the mourners."

When we contemplate a loved one's death—whether it happened recently or a long time ago, and whether that person was old or young—we need comfort. Death is unfathomable. Grappling with its reality is part of the human condition. And when a friend loses a loved one, we need to comfort them. That's part of being a friend and being a member of a community. We will look closely at each of these situations in this chapter. Our wisdom practice offers us guidance for both of them. It shows us a way to respond to loss in a way that ultimately brings meaning and peace.

When a Loved One Dies

Losing a loved one is intensely personal. We feel different about the death of a parent with whom we spoke every day than about coworkers we barely knew. We respond differently to the death of a loved one at fifty-five than to the death of a loved one at ninety-five. The personal feeling attached to mourning often leads us to turn inward. When a close friend or relative dies, few people understand our unique pain. So we feel alone. One common feeling people report to me is numbness, even when the death was expected.

That's why we need our wisdom practices. It fights isolation and encourages empathy. We stand with the mourners and "accompany the dead." We do this in two ways. First we bury. We go to the cemetery. We participate in the shoveling of earth. That does not have to feel gruesome. It is an act of kindness because it shows we take care of our loved one. Its sheer physicality adds to its healing power. It's a concrete act we can do. We ensure a person is properly buried. I tell mourners that they are performing an act of kindness that can never be repaid. It is done purely out of love or respect. That is the physical part of accompanying the dead.

Then we accompany them on a spiritual level. The week after death is a fragile time. Judaism does not have the same idea of purgatory or heaven and hell as other faiths. The sages believed, however, that the souls of the deceased *need* us to help them attain peace in the afterlife. They rely on our prayers to get them to the next stage of existence. In other words, our actions as mourners affect the future of the deceased. That is an extraordinary responsibility.

The chief way we meet it is through a practice known as sitting shivah. Sitting shivah is having people in our homes, praying with them, and sharing memories of the deceased. The mourners are rarely left alone. People are coming and going all the time. I've noticed that no one locks their doors during the seven-day shivah period, and it is rarely thought necessary for a guest to ring the doorbell or call in advance. It is an ongoing open house.

The wisdom behind this practice may seem counterintuitive at first. Why should we feel as if we have to entertain people right after our husband or father has died? Because shivah forces us out of ourselves. It brings us out of the land of the dead back into the land of the living. When a loved one dies, we can feel cut off from life. Even if we have deep faith and believe in an afterlife, we still ask ourselves what the point of living is if it inevitably ends in death. I've seen it hundreds of times. Unexpected losses make it even worse. Normal human activity seems like a burden, and even pointless. I've met with men and women whose spouses died unexpectedly, and they stop eating for days. They rarely leave home.

Shivah makes sure that does not happen. It reintegrates us with life. The hugs we receive, the words of memory shared, the generosity of the people who bring us food—they remind us of the meaningfulness of life. Shivah does not rush us back into everyday activity. Rather, it nudges us back into real community. It focuses on what matters most in this life—our relationships.

A hint of this true purpose of shivah is found in another common practice: the covering of all the mirrors in the home of the mourners. The traditional explanation for this practice is that mirrors symbolize personal vanity, which we should avoid during times of mourning. That may be true. But a lack of mirrors also makes us less tempted to focus on ourselves. It gets out of our heads and into the arms of others.

The practice is powerful. I have never talked to a person or family who regretted having observed shivah. The opposite, however, is often true. One friend lost his wife tragically when she was thirty-two, leaving him with four young children. The oldest were in fifth grade. He thought shivah would be too burdensome for the kids and sent them back to school so they could be distracted from the pain. As he later told me, he did not realize how jarring that would be. He did not appreciate the time it would take for them to feel any sense of normality. We cannot jump right back from the land of the dead into the land of the living. Restoring ourselves takes time. And it takes others dedicated to that process. When we do it well, we arrive in the land of the living with a meaning and perspective that once seemed impossible.

Facebook Teaches Us How to Mourn

In 2015 and 2016 we saw the way this works in the experience of Sheryl Sandberg. Sandberg is a senior executive of Facebook. She helped build it into one of the most influential companies in the world. She achieved tremendous financial success and wrote a (controversial) best-selling book called *Lean In* about how women can find success in work and family. Her husband, Dave Goldberg, was equally accomplished and respected in the tech world. Then, while running on a treadmill, he had a heart attack and died. He was forty-seven.

Much of Sandberg's mourning unfolded on Facebook as she followed the Jewish tradition of sitting shivah. She received visits from friends and strangers. They shared their memories with her. They made sure she was never alone. And when she completed the shivah process, a different perspective was evident. As she wrote, "When life sucks you under, you can kick against the bottom, break the surface, and breathe again. I learned that in the face of the void—or in the face of any challenge—*you can choose joy and meaning*." You can even arrive, she wrote, at "deeper gratitude—gratitude for the kindness of friends, the love of family, the laughter of children." Sitting shivah teaches lessons no other experience can.

Mourning—even simply supporting another person's mourning—can also clarify what matters most. Life is filled with distraction. Websites, books, notifications, and e-mails compete for our attention. Sources of entertainment compete for our dollars. We struggle to figure out where to put our most precious asset—our time. We can make more money. We can produce more food. But we can never make more time. Encountering death brings this truth to our full awareness. The experience encourages us to ponder—sometimes unconsciously—how to make the most of the time that remains.

It is not always easy. Psalm 23 asks God to help us "walk *through* the valley of the shadow of death" (emphasis mine). We cannot walk around it or jump over it. We go through it. That can feel impossible. But when we get through it, we find greater awareness of the fragility of life and a better understanding of ourselves. Sheryl Sandberg described the process of mourning as one in which "you will figure out who you really are—and you just might become the very best version of yourself."

I learned a lot from Sandberg's reflections on mourning. They echoed much of what I've heard from the hundreds of families I have shepherded through the challenges of grief and mourning. Perhaps the most important lesson is not to put any kind of filter on our pain. We need to feel it and not try to suppress our tears. God did not create us with the capacity to feel so that we would avoid using it.

One of the ways we can acknowledge our pain is by writing down our feelings. It helps us find meaning in them. As Viktor Frankl taught us, pain helps us discern meaning. It is also a way of coping. It helps us clarify the way the deceased mattered to us.

When I struggled to find ways to guide my congregants through loss and mourning, I came across the work of Dr. James W. Pennebaker. He was among the first scholars to focus on the therapeutic role of writing. One of his studies found that the stress levels of those writing about their grief decreased markedly. Weeks and months later, those who regularly wrote their feelings in a journal after a loss reported a better mood, a more positive outlook on life, and better physical health.

After reading this, I bought dozens of small journals to give out to mourners. Using guiding questions, we developed a writing plan. Their experience proved the truth of Dr. Pennebaker's research. One congregant who wrote to me said that the writing helped her see more depth in her mother's life. She'd found beauty in the brokenness of her loss. The writing coaxed her back into the world with a renewed sense of purpose and spirit.

Martin Seligman's research also helps us understand why this practice works. Writing lets us reframe our experience. It gives us a feeling of control over how we respond to our loss. We cannot control the fact that we lost someone. But writing helps us control the way we respond to and think about it.

It also gives us a way to map out and record the changes we undergo. Loss shapes us whether we realize it or not. We can become more impatient or more loving, needier or more giving. I have witnessed relationships deteriorate because one partner thought the other, who had just lost her father, was taking too long to "get over it." Writing down our feelings brings them to greater awareness. We can better explain to our partner or friends why we may not be as present as they would like us to be. We can even shape our future emotions by writing down how we hope to feel and envisioning that feeling regularly.

Perhaps the greatest gift writing gives after a loss is that it allows for the untangling of complex emotions. *Sometimes loss is not accompanied only by sadness. Sometimes it comes with relief.* If a loved one has been sick or in pain for a long time, death can feel welcome. But that relief mingles with guilt and anguish. Writing gives us the space to wrestle with those feelings. It is open ended. We do not have to sum it up neatly. We can simply deposit our thoughts and feelings. Writing may not bring closure, but it can help us get out of the grip of grief and guilt.

Something We All Need

Comforting mourners clearly helps the mourners. But how does it make the comforter happier? How does it add to our own well-being in such a way that it is part of the happiness prayer? I've already named what I think is the core gift given to those who comfort mourners: clarification of what matters most. Even if we did not know the deceased, attending to another person's mourning can be a memento mori, a reminder of death: it can push us to devote ourselves to the things that really matter, and to set aside distractions.

But comforters receive other gifts as well. Comforting a mourner both honors our relationship with the mourner and cements that relationship—in other words, a mourner's true friends are the ones who show up, and when we comfort those in mourning, they rarely forget.

About thirty years ago a member of my congregation lost her husband. He had been a successful attorney, active in politics and civic life. He had a sudden heart attack while on a business trip and died almost immediately. Before his death, their phone had never stopped ringing. After he died, it was silent. Many people did come to the funeral, she told me, but few stayed in her life afterward. One couple, however, whom she did not know very well, continued to check in. They invited her out for meals. They went with her to synagogue. They listened to her cry. These acts cemented a friendship that lasts to this day.

Being that kind of friend will make us feel more connected to others. It will bring us the kind of *shalom*, integrity, that enriches life. Now, we cannot be that kind of friend for everybody. Only eight or ten people can really fit around a deathbed. That's a good yardstick for determining the people with whom we can really share our deepest vulnerabilities. We can aim to be a true friend to eight to ten people. Once we've got that, we've got all we need. All of us should aim to find them. These are the people whom we could call at two in the morning knowing they would drop everything to be there for us. Do you have ten people for whom you would do that? Do you know ten people who would do that for you?

If not—and that's the case for many of us—comforting mourners is a chance to invest more in our relationships. This need applies to men and women equally, though I have noticed men pursue these relationships less often than women. Sometimes a rabbi or pastor serves as the two a.m. friend, and that's part of our responsibility. But being a two a.m. friend is about more than two a.m. It is about sharing our vulnerabilities with one another and supporting one another through them. Having and being that kind of friend makes our lives deeper and, ultimately, happier.

We cannot be a two a.m. friend for everyone. And we cannot expect everyone to be a two a.m. friend for us. But our wisdom practice does not say we comfort only our close friends. We mourn in and with our community. One of my favorite scenes in *The Godfather* depicts a funeral service in a small town in Sicily. The entire town is walking from the church to the cemetery. They are accompanying the coffin and mourning as a community. That was the custom for much of history. Comforting mourners was an individual and communal responsibility. People made sacrifices to comfort mourners even if they were not close friends.

We see a few remnants of this communal feeling today. Obituaries are often the most popular section of local papers. We allow funeral processions to violate traffic laws by traveling together through red lights. When we see such a procession, we cannot help but notice that a person in our community has died.

For Whom Do We Mourn?

No rule applies in all situations, but in general we try to be present for friends and community members. At my synagogue, our board members attend the funerals of members of the synagogue, even if they do not know them. Initially their presence can surprise the families of the deceased, especially if the funeral is small. They wonder who these strangers are. When I explain, however, some have tears in their eyes. They see a community present for its members. They see a community helping to restore them to life. When we comfort those whom we do not know well, we send a message that the world cares about them. The deceased, we are silently saying, mattered more than their survivors know.

Our presence can also symbolize God's presence. One of the most powerful texts in the Talmud asks what it means to say, as the Bible does, that human beings are created "in the image of God." The sages answer, "Just as God welcomes the stranger, so shall we. Just as God clothes the naked, so shall we. And just as God comforts mourners, so shall we." We make God's invisible presence visible when we are there for one another.

How do we comfort effectively? Many books have been written on this question. One of the overriding imperatives is not to talk to the mourners with false optimism. Repeatedly saying, "Everything is going to be okay" immediately after a death tends to be counterproductive. It reflects our own lack of comfort with death and loss, rather than an attention to the interests of the mourner. Even when the loss is expected, the mourner still experiences the world differently. A loss is a loss, and the world will never be the same for the mourner. Not acknowledging that truth makes us seem insincere.

I have found that the best way to start is to acknowledge the feeling of pain, loss, and even anger. Saying, "This is just awful" or "This is a big loss" tells the mourner you recognize they have experienced a significant event. You can also say, "I'm sorry for your loss." It acknowledges the experience without substituting your perception of the way the mourner is feeling. Then you can say, "Tell me about your dad/mom/brother/sister." You give the mourner the chance to say as little or as much as they want about the deceased. You are signaling a willingness to listen and a concern for the deceased. When you listen, you show you are not going through the motions. You are present. And then you listen.

Listening Is a Superpower

Listening reveals a power inside us. A friend who is a rabbi in California used a beautiful analogy to describe it. The analogy is based on a quotation attributed to Michelangelo. When asked how he created his celebrated sculpture of King David, he said, "Every block of stone has a sculpture inside of it, and it is the task of the sculptor to discover it." Similarly, this rabbi suggested that there is a wellspring of empathy and kindness inside each of us. Our unique task is to discover it. Listening is one of ways we do so. So is each of the other wisdom practices that make up our prayer.

As we follow them, we see their influence not only in the practices themselves, but also throughout our lives. As an example, as we do more to comfort mourners, we see positive changes in our relationships with our family. Our kindness at home encourages more generosity at work. Goodness builds on itself. The same is true in the other parts of life. People who start exercising, for example, often report their eating habits and work productivity also improve. The practices in this book are not ends in themselves. They shape our characters. And that process never ends.

That's one of the lessons taught by a seminal rabbi in the

1930s and early 1940s. He came from a town in Poland called Piaseczno. Thus, he was known as the Piaseczno Rebbe (*rebbe* is an affectionate term for a rabbi). Piaseczno is near Warsaw, and when the Jews of Warsaw and the surrounding communities were imprisoned by the Nazis in a tiny ghetto, he became known as the Rabbi of the Warsaw Ghetto.

He was forbidden from leading prayers in the ghetto. Teaching classes or speaking Hebrew was punishable by death. But every day he would meet with children terrified by the war and the Nazis. Those who survived the Warsaw Ghetto (about two hundred out of eighty thousand) described him as the children's father, mother, and best friend. The rebbe himself died after the Nazis sent all the Jews in the ghetto to the death camps.

Among his writings is a summary of why we try to follow the practices in our happiness prayer. He said, "Their essence is to reveal our true selves." In other words, following our ten practices releases the potential goodness lying dormant inside us. Once we release it, it reshapes us, bringing us closer to God and to one another. That journey never ends. Like wine that gains flavor and depth as it ages, we human beings grow happier when we continue to comfort mourners and follow the other wisdom practices.

I saw proof of the rebbe's wisdom once after a funeral I conducted. The funeral took place at the graveside. It was a warm day, and many of the assembled lingered at the graveside after the funeral service. As I walked out of the cemetery, I overheard two members of my congregation talking. Both were in their upper eighties. Using morbid humor, one said to the other, "We might as well just stay here and save ourselves a trip." The other replied, "No. We're not ready. But we can stop and get some corned beef sandwiches and bring them over to Lieberman [a nursing home near the cemetery] on our way home."

I recounted this story a few years later when I presided over the funeral of the man who had said these words. He had been one of the kindest, gentlest people I ever met. And, as one of his daughters put it to me, he was "the happiest man in the world."

Pray with Intention
עיון תפלה

"Wonder rather than doubt is the root of all knowledge."
—Abraham Joshua Heschel

In 2006 the author David Foster Wallace gave a commencement address at Kenyon College. He made a familiar observation, but one I had never heard expressed so clearly and poignantly. "In the day-to-day trenches of adult life," he said, "there is actually no such thing as atheism. There is no such thing as not worshiping. Everybody worships. The only choice we get is what to worship."

Worship is like breathing. We all do it. Sometimes we are aware of it. Usually we are not. To worship something is to makes its satisfaction the center of our life. Many people worship themselves. They live by the philosophy reflected in the words of Bart Simpson when he is asked to say grace. He folds his hands and says, "Dear God, we paid for all this stuff ourselves. So thanks for nothing." He probably doesn't realize it, but Bart expresses the perfect prayer for living a miserable life.

Real happiness leads us outward. It leads us to one another: to community and acts of kindness. It also leads us to embrace a power greater than ourselves. Sometimes that power seems faint, distant, and unreachable. Sometimes we even feel that power is acting against us. I sat recently with parents who had lost their twenty-two-year-old son. Their utter pain had turned to anger. How could God let this happen? When I began praying with them, the dad kept shaking his head. "It's too raw, Rabbi. It's too much. I can't say these words." I told him that his tears were his prayer. And God heard them and felt them.

Worship can be a loaded word. So can *prayer*. They bring certain images to mind, usually of someone making a physical motion or kneeling and looking up toward the sky and saying something. But we will see that prayer is much more than that. It is much more than a series of words. It is much more than asking for something. True prayer comes from the heart. It is not just reading words from a page. It is not only repeating a phrase. It is a bubbling forth of what is inside us.

And prayer works. It does not always work the way we think it will. Prayer is not a combination of life insurance and magic. It is not a simple way to solve our problems. It is an acknowledgement that we cannot get through life all alone. It is a way of opening a door for God. When we open that door, we find strength we did not know we had. When we open that door, we discover we are not alone. To open that door, we need first to clear away a few obstacles. Doing so will help us with prayer generally and with deepening our experience of the happiness prayer in particular.

The Wrong Ideas of Prayer

The biggest obstacle to prayer is our own definitions of what it is. We think prayer is mainly about asking God for things.

The comedian Emo Philips satirized this idea in a classic

joke. "When I was a little boy," he said, "I used to pray every night for a new bicycle. Then I realized the Lord in His wisdom doesn't work that way, so I just stole one and asked Him to forgive me."

Prayer is less about asking for what we want than it is about figuring out what we should want. It is aligning our desires with ancient wisdom rather than trying to force God to meet our desires.

Sometimes we imagine that prayer works like a vending machine. We put something in. We get something out. If nothing happens, we think that either God just said no, or we're not worthy enough to merit God's attention. But successful prayer does not always change our circumstances. It changes us. And the prayers that change us are often not the formal ones we say in a church or synagogue. They are the words of hope we say and tears of pain we shed in private. They are the text messages we send to friends in need. Prayer brings our attention to what matters most. And when we are truly engrossed in prayer, we get out of our own way. We empty ourselves of ourselves. Practiced consistently over time, prayer nurtures gratitude rather than resentment. It lets us set aside the emotional baggage blocking us from God and from one another. We create a space for God, and God dwells where we let Him in. In prayer, God changes us.

What Is Prayer?

How do we make that space for God to change us? How do we follow this wisdom practice of praying with intention? First we listen. Prayer begins with listening. The Hebrew word for "listening" is *shema*. But in biblical Hebrew, *shema* means much more than listening in the auditory sense. It refers to internalizing, responding, obeying, doing. The King James Bible used an old English word to translate *shema*: that word is *hearken*. When we pray, we hearken to God's voice not just with our ears, but also with our mind, heart, and body.

Listening with full attention takes great effort. How often do we talk with our friends and family and listen only for what we want to hear? How often do we seem to listen to someone when we are really waiting for our chance to speak? How many of us have talked on the phone and read e-mail at the same time? To listen attentively is to be truly present, and it can be a struggle.

To listen to God—whose voice is not audible—is even harder. The sages teach this truth in a wonderful story about the burning bush. Moses, you'll recall, saw a bush in the desert that was burning but not being consumed by the flames. The sages said that before Moses, many people had passed that bush. God's voice spoke out continuously from it. But only Moses had the heart to stop and hear it. As one rabbi put it, "The miracle was not that God called out to Moses from a burning bush. The miracle was that Moses heard Him." Hearing often requires more of the heart than of the eardrum.

Prayer is not only listening. It is also conversation. Praying ancient words is a time-tested formula for talking with God. Again, we do not talk to God to get something. We talk to God to be transformed through the relationship. Martin Buber, whose notion of I–Thou relationships we discussed in earlier chapters, helps us understand how this conversation changes us.

Buber believed that God dwelled in I–Thou relationships. In effect, he said, every I–Thou relationship has a third party: God. We access God through others. For example, when my children came into the world, I felt God's presence in the hospital room. When my grandfather said, "I love you," on his deathbed, God was there. When I said a prayer after asking my wife to marry me, God was there. For Buber, God is the name we give to that feeling of intimacy and connection.

In contrast to Buber, however, I believe God is not just the name we give to that feeling. *God dwells in that connection.* And we can speak to God directly through prayer. That's why we say, "Blessed are You, eternal God," at the beginning of most Jewish prayers.

Now, we are not going to feel God's presence powerfully every time we pray. Great hitters in baseball get on base about once in every three at bats. Great pray-ers may feel a closeness to God one out of five or ten times. Yet over time, God will become a regular presence. Like a friendship that deepens with the years, our relationship with God deepens as we pray. Have you ever noticed that after many years of marriage, each partner becomes like the other? They often smooth out one another's rough edges. That happens in long-term friendships as well. It can even happen when two people work together for a long time. And it happens in prayer. We become different people; it often happens slowly and imperceptibly, but over time the change becomes evident.

I've seen it in my synagogue with members who have attended regularly for fifty years. Somehow they have said the prayers so many times that the prayers have become part of their character. They brim with kindness. You can feel the sincerity in their words. Prayer has shaped them. They are living testimonies of its power.

Prayer is also a way of marking sacred moments. Very often we think about praying during a time of crisis. We know the saying that there are no atheists in foxholes. Some pray only when they need an emergency divine intervention. But prayer can be more than that. Prayer expands our most joyful moments by adding a layer of holiness.

Prayer in a New York Restaurant

About a year ago, I was in my office when a member of the temple came by and asked if we could chat for a minute. We sat down, and he asked me if I knew the words of a blessing he had just heard. He didn't know how it went except that it started with the phrase *Baruch atah Adonai*, "Blessed are You, O God."

"OK," I said, "it could be anything. Can you tell me where you heard it?"

"Yes. I was in New York last week and having dinner at a restaurant. Just a few tables away from me, right as I was eating, a man proposed to his girlfriend. She said yes, and everybody in the restaurant cheered. Then the man walked quietly over to a corner, put on a head covering, and said some type of blessing. Both their eyes filled with tears. I barely heard what he said, but it was quite short."

"The blessing," I said, "may have been the Shehecheyanu. Did it go like this: *Baruch atah Adonai Eloyhanu melech haolam shechyanu, v'keemanu v'heegeyanu l'zeman hazeh*? The words mean, 'Blessed are You, O God, sovereign of the universe, for giving us life, for sustaining us, and for enabling us to reach this joy-filled moment.'"

He said, "That's it! Do you have a copy of it?" "Yes, absolutely," I said. "Good," he said. "I am planning to propose to my girlfriend this weekend, and I want to say it with her."

Unbeknownst to them, the couple in the New York restaurant released powerful sparks that transformed another's life. A blessing of gratitude became a source of inspiration. Blessings express our feelings. They are words that come from the heart. And as the great Jewish sages taught, "Words from the heart enter the heart."

Can Prayer Make Us Happier?

Now we know what prayer is. But how does it work? How does it make us happier?

Prayer is different for everyone. The feelings I bring to prayer are different from those you will bring. But God is big enough for both of us. One of the ways I picture God hearing prayer is like water being poured over ice. If you fill a glass with ice and then pour water into it, the water touches all the ice cubes. But it touches them in different places and in different ways. In prayer we are the ice cubes. God is the water. God's spirit hits each of us differently. You might leave the prayer filled with gratitude. I might leave brimming with hope. Someone else might leave with greater acceptance.

Over time, however, all of us will leave with greater happiness and perspective. As we see from the work of Professor T. M. Luhrmann of Stanford University, people who pray regularly report greater satisfaction with life. They are more likely than those who don't pray to see purpose in their lives and meaning in their deeds. Luhrmann focuses in particular on prayer as an intimate conversation with God. She reported that those who prayed saw God as a friend who understood them. Those in her study showed more robust immune systems and decreases in blood pressure. Her work has given scholarly depth to what has often been portrayed as a simplistic practice.

Prayer also focuses our minds. When done consistently, prayer has a similar impact on the brain to meditation, which has been shown to make us calmer and more patient and compassionate. This positive effect of prayer does not come from some magical power. It comes from consistency. Like water that slowly smooths out a rock on a beach by washing over it day after day, prayer smooths our rough edges as we do it day after day. Prayers are not just lofty thoughts uttered in big words. They express real human emotions.

They also add meaning to our lives. They give contours to our life story because words of prayer make us more emotionally aware and intelligent. They push us to ask ourselves if we are living up to the hopes and visions expressed in them. They challenge us to see whether we are living up to our commitments, our relationships, our aspirations. They add to our emotional vocabulary by exposing us to the dreams, hopes, pains, and yearnings of those who came before us.

That is what happened to me with the happiness prayer. I knew in theory the meaning and purpose of prayer. I had been praying since I could speak. But with the happiness prayer, *I decided to go where the prayer took me.* So every day after I said it in the morning, I would write my immediate reactions in my journal. That usually took about three minutes. Sometimes my thoughts were reflections on some way I'd applied a few of the wisdom practices from the prayer the day before. Sometimes I expressed guilt about not doing more. The point was that I was putting my attention on the words of the prayer.

Then I would write down three ways I would fulfill the wisdom practices from the prayer that day. Would I take time to study? Would I call my parents? Would I do something to comfort someone who had lost a relative or friend? Now, some of the practices fall within the purview of my job. So I would deliberately try to stretch myself by doing at least one thing that had nothing to do with my work.

I discovered that the most important part of my day was the decision to let the happiness prayer guide my life. It became a filter for what to say and what to do. And in letting it guide me, I not only felt happier, I also actually felt greater control. I had clarity about the next right thing to do. It was like going to the supermarket and knowing exactly the healthy foods to get rather than feeling tempted by everything in sight. There are so many things we pray for. But the happiness prayer is something we live for.

It took a while for me to notice the change it made in my life. But others noticed it sooner. "You're smiling more when you speak," my wife told me. The president of the congregation even noticed that I was sitting up straighter. Sometimes our body begins to process change before our mind does. That happened to me. The happiness prayer does not create overnight change. And I'm glad it doesn't. Instant change, like New Year's resolutions, rarely lasts. It is the slow, steady, incremental improvements in ourselves that truly shape us. That's what happens when we live the happiness prayer.

How to Be a Better Pray-er

A few other factors shaped my experience with the happiness prayer, and they can enrich our experience of prayer more generally. The first is praying with other people. In Judaism most prayer happens in groups because communal prayer bonds us with others. A prayer group in Judaism must consist of at least ten people. That group is known as a minyan. Part of the reason we pray in a group is that it helps us feel accountable to others. People notice if we do not show up for prayer; therefore we feel more obligated to do so. We can pray by ourselves. Many of us do regularly. But praying as a community gives us support and positive peer pressure.

It also magnifies the power of prayer. Prayer in a community brings us face-to-face with other people. We can't escape to our own thoughts and rationalizations. Looking around at others, we need to ask ourselves if we are living up to the ideals expressed in our prayers. Are we showing kindness? Are we treating others as we wish to be treated? Are we living a life that makes a difference? Communal prayer uses the power of group dynamics.

In addition to praying with others, we also need to get into the right mind-set. Prayer is not about a catechism. It is not simply reciting what we believe. It never was. It is about saying words and gathering together to live better and *to experience God* in our midst. The first prayers were probably uttered at moments similar to the ones at which we say spontaneous prayers now—times of great joy or fear. When we recognize that prayer is intensely human—and not something just for the church or synagogue—we feel more comfortable with it.

As we begin to feel more comfortable with prayer, we can get past what I often see as a final stumbling block: picturing God. Doing this may not be a problem for believers. But experience and the many questions congregants ask me suggest it is a powerful concern for some because many of the traditional descriptions of God do not resonate for people today. Many of the biblically based prayers, for example, see God as a king. Kings were the most powerful figures in the world of the ancient Near East, the world of the Bible. As the greatest power in the universe, God was seen as the king of kings. This view found its way into almost every prayer. Most Jewish blessings, for example, begin with the words "Blessed are You, O God, sovereign of the universe."

The idea of God as a king, however, does not speak to many people today—at least in North America. Since many of us have no experience of kings, this idea may paradoxically make God seem less relevant and meaningful. *We need language to describe God that speaks to our hearts and minds.*

I like to think of God as the breath of life. We know we need to breathe in order to live. In other words, without breath, we cannot live. Without God, the universe and everything that is in it cannot live. God also embodies goodness. We want to be closer to God by living as God would want us to live. God forgives, so we should forgive. God takes care of us, so we should act with kindness toward one another. The happiness prayer draws on this understanding of God and reminds us who God is so we can remind ourselves who we can be.

And we grow into our best selves as we pray because we gain more control over our attention and focus. Neuropsychologist Rick Hanson defines prayer as "meditation in the presence of something transcendent." While people of faith may find this definition insufficient, it captures a significant dimension of prayer. That dimension is the focusing of attention. To meditate on something is to give it our attention. When we pray, we meditate on God's words. The sustained attention we give those words can, as Hanson writes, improve our moods and make our brains more elastic. When we pray as a community and with communal singing, the voices and presence of others can reinforce our focus. Have you ever felt moved to sing along with a group? The same positive encouragement happens in prayer.

Silent or quiet prayer in which we meditate on or quietly repeat particular words or phrases also makes us happier. Several studies, most notably the one done by Dr. Herbert Benson, a cardiovascular specialist at Harvard Medical School and a leader in the field of mind/body medicine, illustrate what he calls "the relaxation response." As written in a Huffington Post article on Dr. Benson's findings, during prayer and meditation, "The body's metabolism decreases, the heart rate slows, blood pressure goes down, and our breath becomes calmer and more regular." In other words, prayer calms the body. It alters our moods. The words grease the neural pathways of our minds, leading us to greater comfort and well-being.

Now, some may wonder whether simple meditation and breathing exercises can be just as effective as prayer in promoting happiness and presence. Perhaps. Each of us is different. *Prayer, however, is more than our being present. It also brings us into the presence of God.*

When we are present and God is present, prayer becomes the bridge keeping us connected. Sometimes we speak and God listens. Sometimes God speaks and we listen. We cannot see God or touch God, but we can be present with God in the way lovers can be present with one another even when they are not in the same room.

Three Types of Prayer

Prayer probably began when our human ancestors felt great emotion and cried out to God. Over time, however, many of these spontaneous prayers were written down. Along with many other Jewish prayers, the happiness prayer was written down about two thousand years ago. The Jewish sages eventually assembled a book containing the prayers they saw as most important. These traditional prayers have been proven to stimulate our hearts and minds, and they have withstood the test of time. Sometimes we find it easier to look at words people have said before us, especially when it is difficult to find the right words to express our feelings.

The Jewish prayer book contains three types of traditional prayers. The first is prayers of praise. They describe God's greatness. Such prayers of praise are not for God's benefit; God does not have an ego that needs to be stroked. In praising God, however, we remind ourselves of our own limitations. We remind ourselves that the universe is full of gifts we did nothing to merit. We stand in awe of the world and its creator. We use the gifts we were given—the ability to speak, to listen, to praise—to express our gratitude. As Rabbi David J. Wolpe put it, "In praising God, we come to understand that all we can offer to God is what God has given us: voice, heart, soul. We work with God's marvelous gift to exalt its Giver. That is why every praise of God also leads to thanks."

Giving thanks is the purpose of the second type of prayer—prayers of gratitude. This type of prayer is the most common in the Jewish prayer book. We already saw in an earlier chapter the way gratitude adds to our happiness. Prayers of gratitude help keep it foremost in our minds. They also reflect our human need to express, give thanks for, and focus our attention on the many ways we are indebted to others. We are indebted to our parents for our lives. We are indebted to the teachers who helped us learn. If we ever ride in a car, we are indebted to the scientists who developed the combustion engine and the engineers who put together the car. Prayers of gratitude help us live with continual thanks.

The third type of prayer is the prayer of petition. Prayers

of petition are ones in which we ask God to do things. These things can be specific or general. In the traditional Jewish prayer book, for example, is a prayer asking God for rain for the fields. That is a specific request. We may also ask for more general benefits like greater wisdom or less anxiety or more self-control. In our own relationship with God, we ask for particular things. I sometimes ask God to help me feel a connection to my congregation and inspire them with a good sermon during the holidays.

Can You Surprise Yourself?

We can pray in our own words or in the words millions of others have prayed before us. Either way can bring satisfaction when the prayer speaks to and clarifies what we live for. Sometimes, however, the traditional prayers—such as the Lord's Prayer for Christians or the Shema for Jews—trigger an unexpected and powerful feeling. They nurture what the great rabbi and theologian Abraham Joshua Heschel called the most important quality of a satisfying spiritual life: the ability to be surprised.

That has certainly been true for me. I didn't know the effect the happiness prayer would have on my life. But I let it guide me. When we say the prayers with openness to the range of meanings of their words, they lead us down unanticipated paths of memory and gratitude.

Sometimes the meanings we derive from prayers have little to do with their original purpose. But that's OK. Prayer can be a form of emotional exploration. For example, one of the morning prayers in Judaism asks God to gather the exiles of the Jewish people back to the land of Israel; the prayer was written two thousand years ago by Jews exiled from Jerusalem by the

Roman emperor. Eventually, around 135 CE, Rome banned all Jews from Jerusalem, though a tiny group remained. Jewish life began to flourish outside the land of Israel in places like Babylonia, Spain, and France. Still, the prayer asking God to return us to the land of Israel persisted. It expressed a feeling of nostalgia and a longing for a time of independence and prosperity. More broadly, it reflected an emotion many of us feel when we think about "the good ol' days," times when things seemed easier.

When I say this prayer for return, though, I don't usually think about returning to Israel. I think of my grandfather. I think of the migration of his parents to America and the way they created a new life here. I see the hand of God in their deciding to uproot themselves from Europe and create a new life far away. This imagery does not fit with the origins and words of the prayer. But for me its words trigger not nostalgia, but gratitude.

Is it wrong to feel this way? It is wrong to feel something totally out of sync with the literal words of a prayer? Not when we see prayer as a means of emotional exploration. Not when we realize prayer can trigger associations we never imagined. The ancient words of prayer matter because they lend themselves to different feelings. They are like great literature. Every generation can see parts of itself in their words.

Ultimately, though prayer consists of words, its influence extends beyond words. It shapes our behavior. It shapes our values. Those of us who emerge from prayer as transformed people know how powerful it can be. It not only helps us become more mindful and happier individuals, but also helps us cultivate the graciousness and ethical sensibility toward which God consistently directs us.

Forgive

הבאת שלום בין אדם לחברו

"Forgiveness is the key to action and freedom."
—Hannah Arendt

All of us have been hurt by other people. Perhaps a friend betrayed a secret. Perhaps a teacher told us we didn't have what it takes. Perhaps a partner squandered our trust. We have also hurt others and seen others get hurt. But life offers opportunities for redemption. The key is forgiveness.

The big challenge is that forgiveness is rarely easy. I have sat with hundreds of people struggling with it. Among my greatest guides in finding the strength to forgive and offering insight to those struggling with the challenge is a book published sixty years ago. Entitled *Peace of Mind: Insights on Human Nature That Can Change Your Life*, it came from the pen of Rabbi Joshua Loth Liebman. He brought Jewish wisdom and psychological insight to bear on the challenges facing returning World War II veterans and their growing families.

In a world still trying to find peace among nations, Rabbi Loth Liebman argued that real peace does not come only from politics. Peace begins inside each of us. Peace is not what happens "out there." Peace begins in our hearts, in our relationships, in our families, and in our communities.

I first read the book in 2001. It articulated so much of what I loved about Judaism and brought me closer to God and my calling. Then, in 2004, when my grandmother died, my mom and I found a copy of the book in a box in her basement. Dozens of paragraphs were underlined. Seeing them gave me one of those rare moments in life when we encounter God's fingerprints. My grandmother—who had suffered from illness for most of the time I knew her—had shared my interests and passion.

In rereading *Peace of Mind* as I was living the happiness prayer, I asked myself what Rabbi Liebman would have to say to those of us in the twenty-first century searching for greater happiness and well-being. He would, I think, focus on the ninth wisdom practice—forgiveness. Rabbi Liebman may even have been writing a sequel to *Peace of Mind*, focusing on finding peace in relationships, when he died suddenly of a heart attack in 1948. He said one of the critical imperatives of meaningful relationships—and one of most effective ways of getting greater peace of mind—is forgiveness.

What Is Forgiveness?

Almost everyone I know has issues with forgiveness. We either can't forgive someone who hurt us, or we are frustrated someone can't forgive us. But many of our struggles stem from a misunderstanding of forgiveness. We associate it with apology. We think it's simply a matter of saying, "I'm sorry." Then it's up to the other party to accept our apology.

We may also associate forgiveness with wiping the slate

clean. This association derives from the meaning of forgiveness in financial terms. When a bank loan is forgiven, we don't need to pay any money back. Our balance sheet is clear. Thus we assume forgiveness in our relationships means clearing the slate. The relationship is restored to what it once was. Some people even think forgiveness is condoning. When we forgive, this approach says, we recognize what happened was not really a big deal.

But forgiveness is none of these things. Forgiveness is not condoning. It is not simply apologizing or accepting an apology. It is not restoring a relationship to what it once was. *To ask for forgiveness is to accept responsibility.* It is to say, "Yes, it was my fault. Now I see that I was wrong. I apologize and resolve to act differently." Seeking forgiveness includes remorse along with regret. It is not appeasement. It is reconciliation.

Reconciliation does not require forgetting. It does, however, demand we give up on animosity and the desire for revenge. Forgiveness takes courage. The desire for revenge is a natural human instinct, and forgiveness demands we tame that instinct. Perhaps this recognition is why this wisdom practice is included among our ten. As with all our other practices, the benefits of following it are enormous. *Forgiving is itself a form of revenge!* We no longer let the other party have a hold on our hearts and minds. It is a favor we do ourselves because it releases energies we would have expended in feeling hurt and aggrieved.

The First Recorded Act of Forgiveness

The Bible contains the first example of forgiveness in recorded history. But we go through a lot of hostile relationships before we get to it. Cain kills Abel. Abraham banishes his son Ishmael.

Jacob steals the birthright from his brother Esau. But then we come to Joseph.

Joseph was sold into slavery by his jealous brothers. He almost died in prison, but then he rose to great power. He saw his brothers again after twenty years. And he forgave them. First, however, they admitted responsibility. Then they asked for forgiveness. They used the Hebrew word for forgiveness for the first time in the Bible, saying, "Now please forgive the sins of the servants of the God of your father." When Joseph heard this request, he wept. The cycle of violence had been stopped. That's part of what forgiveness does. Imagine a world in which we never forgave. Conflicts would never end. Friends and spouses would hold continuous grudges. God used Joseph to give a great gift to humanity.

But it's not only Joseph who teaches us. So do his brothers. They had the courage to *ask* for forgiveness. That changed them. To find forgiveness is to begin anew. One eighteenth-century rabbi went so far as to say that one who has sinned, repented, and been forgiven is closer to God than someone who has only been righteous. To be forgiven is to receive a great gift. It also makes life more manageable.

What Forgiveness Takes

That is the message of a Jewish folktale about a poor man who wandered from town to town with a heavy load of all his earthly possessions on his back. A wagon driver saddled up next to him and offered to give him a ride to the next town. The relieved pauper complied. After a few miles, the wagon driver stopped for a rest. He looked back into his wagon and saw that the man was still carrying the load on his back. He asked, "Why are you still carrying your load? You can put it down in the wagon!"

The pauper responded, "Dear sir, you have been so kind to offer me a ride. I cannot possibly impose upon you to ask you to carry my heavy load as well."

God carries the whole world, and still we think that we have to carry it ourselves. Letting go releases a burden that has been loading us down. We can let it go. Few acts add more to our satisfaction and well-being.

But we can understand why the pauper hesitated in releasing his burden. We do not like to admit to having been wrong. Over time many of us learn how to admit mistakes. We have to do so in order to get along with others. But that training goes against what our earliest and deepest instincts tell us. If you observe little children, you'll see it takes several years before they realize not everything they do is justified. The ability to forgive takes time to teach children—as well as ourselves.

Indeed, one of the reasons Joseph is a hero is that we know how difficult it can be to forgive. Sometimes we have to look closely at ourselves so we can see what is standing in our way. A rabbinic colleague shared with me the following story. A member of his congregation named Daniel was cleaning out his late mother's attic. He found a box of calendars. His mom had always been meticulous and saved them. This box contained her daily planners from 1948 through 1997!

Every day had its list of tasks. Most of them were checked off. Occasionally those left incomplete were circled. Beginning in 1955, every October 22 had the task "Call Sylvia." It was always circled.

Sylvia was his mom's sister-in-law. They'd had a falling out. Every October 22, which was Sylvia's birthday, Daniel's mom had intended to call her and make amends. She never did.

Then in 1987, one of the tasks listed and checked off for October 22 was "Visited Sylvia at the cemetery. Told her I was sorry."

That is a sad story with a real truth. We resist seeking and offering forgiveness. We do not want to lose face or show our vulnerability. I suspect Daniel's mom understood she bore some culpability for the falling-out between her and Sylvia. She resisted forgiving herself for whatever she'd done. Her energy remained focused on resisting any admission of guilt; thus she did not have the fortitude to seek forgiveness from Sylvia, even though she had the will to do so. We can want something but not want to do the hard work necessary to attain it.

The hard work Daniel's mom had to do was forgiving herself. It sounds easier than it is. We can live a long time without looking closely at ourselves. We can simply rationalize our mistakes rather than let something go and move on. One reason we resist forgiving ourselves is that we are uncomfortable with our imperfections. We feel we have to be perfect—or at least present ourselves as perfect. This can hurt our relationships, as it did with Daniel's mother and her sister-in-law. Forgiving ourselves lets us look at the past with empathy rather than frustration. We can even enjoy the process. As Thomas Moore put it in *The Soul's Religion: Cultivating a Profoundly Spiritual Way of Life*, "I have made many mistakes and done a lot of foolish things, but when I look back at the person I was, I feel affection for him."

When we forgive ourselves, we feel better seeking forgiveness from others. When we have come to terms with ourselves, we can acknowledge who we have been to others. We can speak with integrity about our past and seek forgiveness for any harm we have done.

There is no three- or ten-step program for seeking forgiveness. We can start, however, by asking ourselves some critical questions. Answering these questions helps us discover *why* we should want to forgive. Knowing the *why* makes us more likely to learn and pursue the *how*.

First Questions

Psychologists know that emotions drive us more than reason. Therefore, creating an emotional push for forgiveness can lead us to pursue it. We can ask ourselves, "How would being forgiven feel?" We can picture that feeling.

Neuroscientists and psychologists have long known about the power of such imagery. When we picture—in as much detail as possible—how forgiveness would feel, we unconsciously take steps and make changes in our mind-set to help make it happen.

A related question to ask ourselves is, "What kind of future do I envision?" In other words, are we prepared to live in tension with this person for the rest of our lives? Continuous tension repels us. We can avoid it by seeking forgiveness. In doing so, we focus on the future rather than the past. On a factual level, the past is unchangeable. What happened cannot be undone. On the level of meaning, however, the past can be reimagined. What was once understood as an irreparable break in a relationship can become a stumbling block we set aside.

This is the Jewish notion of *teshuvah*, which is sometimes translated as "repentance" but really meaning "turning." *Teshuvah* changes the meaning of the past through what we do in the present. We turn something around and see it in a new way. This is not some mystical, unreasonable idea. We do it all the time. Think about a job you didn't get, and thinking that was the end of the world. Then, a few months later, maybe you got offered an even better position, and recognized that the earlier rejection had been just the push you needed to get the job that was right for you. Or think about a break in a relationship that seemed to doom you to loneliness, before it led you to find a new person who helped you transform your life. Our pasts, like our futures, are not set in stone. Their meaning changes as we change.

The third question to ask yourself is taken from one of the greatest teachers of Jewish history: Hillel. In a section of the Talmud known as "Wisdom of the Ancestors," Hillel offered one of the most quoted gems of Jewish wisdom. "If I am not for myself," he asks, "who will be for me? If I am only for myself, what am I? And if not now, when?"

The first two questions challenge us to balance self-interest with communal responsibility. The third question pushes us to action. That's the one we need when it comes to forgiveness. In effect, it gives us a deadline. And deadlines make us more productive. In the case of forgiveness, the deadline is now.

The problem is that when we have a difficult decision to make, we look for ways to delay. Politicians are masterful at this. But we all do it. We resist going to a doctor until we absolutely have to. We wait until the last minute to book a plane ticket or pay a bill. Ultimately, when it comes to health and finances, circumstances force us to take action. But on softer issues like seeking forgiveness, we can delay without end.

That's what happened to Daniel's mother. She knew she should call her sister-in-law. Yet the consequences of not doing so were not immediate or pressing. She could delay. They became pressing only when Sylvia died, and by then it was too late. That's why we need a deadline. That's why we need to answer Hillel's question. If not now, when?

But even if we do act and ask for forgiveness, we may be rebuffed. Jewish law says we are required to ask three times. If all three attempts are rebuffed, we are forgiven. God forgives us, and it is as if God is standing in as a proxy for the other person. And even when we are rejected by the other party, seeking forgiveness can make us happier because of the satisfaction we gain from recognizing the consequences of our actions.

Alas, we do not only ask for forgiveness. Others also seek it from us. Getting asked for forgiveness can trouble our conscience because we often see forgiving as condoning. We see it as excusing bad behavior or forgetting that something painful happened. Sometimes we even think forgiving another person suggests we hold some measure of fault for their behavior.

This perception is a dangerous one because it misconstrues the purpose of forgiveness. Forgiveness is not something we do for another person. It is something we do for ourselves. As we will soon see, forgiving may not even be the best word for what we need to do when someone who has hurt us asks us to forgive.

A Heartbreaking Story of Pain

I witnessed this truth in an extraordinary encounter during the first year I was intensely living the happiness prayer. I received an e-mail from an acquaintance from college. We were not especially close, but we had lived in the same dormitory for two years. She was not Jewish, but she knew I'd become a rabbi and trusted me and got in touch about twelve years after we graduated. In college she had been an athlete, fit and smart and friendly. She had been the kind of person you picture when you think of Stanford University. But she told me a harrowing story.

In high school she had been beaten by her boyfriend. She was trapped in this abusive relationship for three years until she was able to break it off when she started college. She did not tell anyone about it until after college graduation. She contacted me because she had received an e-mail from her ex-boyfriend. In the e-mail he assumed full responsibility for his battering, and acknowledged that he had caused her pain that had extended beyond the high school years. He didn't try to excuse his behavior—but he did ask her to forgive him.

My acquaintance asked what she should do. Should she grant the forgiveness he was seeking? My initial response was silence. I did not know what to say. She told me she questioned his timing. She had begun to speak more openly about the experience, and she thought word might have gotten back to some of his friends. Maybe he was not genuinely sorry. Perhaps he was asking for forgiveness to stop her from telling more people. I thought for several minutes about what to advise.

The literal Hebrew words of the happiness prayer tell us to "bring about peace [*shalom*] among people." I asked myself how I could do this here. The easy answer would be, "I know this is very hard. What he did continues to hurt and cause pain. But if we can conclude his act of repentance is genuine, you can forgive him and move on." Another easy answer would be, "What he did is unforgivable. You should tell him you despise him and will never forgive him." Neither would really bring about *shalom* because *shalom* is both inner and outer peace.

I thought the first option would not bring her inner peace because she could not really determine whether his remorse was genuine. The second option would not bring outer peace because the tension would remain palpable. But I realized both she and I were thinking about forgiveness in the wrong way. In both these cases, we were focusing on him and his actions. In other words, we were focusing on the perpetrator and the past.

But forgiving is not a favor we do for the person who seeks forgiveness. It is not about relieving another person's feeling of shame or guilt for the past. That is too often the way we think of it because we rely on the financial meaning of forgiveness. When a bank forgives a loan, the loan disappears. We need not think about it anymore. But forgiveness in interpersonal relationships does not work in the same way. Forgiveness is not forgetting or condoning or wiping the slate clean. It is not deciding to relieve someone of responsibility for their actions. Rather, it is letting go of hate, anger, and the desire for revenge. It is refusing to let another person define our feelings.

With this understanding of forgiveness, I told my acquaintance *she had already forgiven him, even if she had not said those words*. She had chosen positive emotions, and she was moving forward with her life and sharing her story. How he interpreted her behavior was his issue, not hers. She had already done the hard work because she had moved on. That is forgiveness, and it was a gift she had given herself.

The benefits of such an act are immense. The eloquent priest and writer Richard Rohr makes this point explicitly when he writes, "Forgiveness is simply the religious word for letting go. To forgive readily is to let go of the negative story line, the painful story line.... If that story line has become your identity, if you are choosing to live in a victim state, an abused consciousness, it gives you a false kind of power." Forgiveness is a gift we give ourselves. It changes our story and ensures we are traveling forward in our lives rather than backward. When we move on, we open up our world and our future. My friend had already let go. She had already found the inner *shalom*. She did not need to do more.

Now you might rightfully say to me, "What about the guy? He asked for forgiveness. If she had moved on, shouldn't she just tell him she forgives him?" The truth is that his forgiveness does not depend on her. His inner peace does not depend on her. It depends on him. He can be forgiven without her telling him she has forgiven him, if he truly repents and takes responsibility for his actions.

Maimonides, the great eleventh- and twelfth-century rabbi, taught this truth when he explained the meaning of repenting and taking responsibility for our actions. We know we have repented when we face a situation similar to the one in which we previously sinned, and we act differently. When we have the opportunity to commit the sin again and do not, we have repented.

Now, in this man's case, he cannot return to high school and recreate the situation with my friend. If he has, however, confessed his sin and consciously entered into other relationships and shown full respect for his partner and clearly changed, he has begun the path of repentance. One way he could show full recognition and make up for some of the harm he cannot undo would be to contribute funds to or volunteer at a shelter for victims of domestic violence. Again, this would not absolve him of responsibility for what he once did. It would, however, create a path to change. The gates of forgiveness are always open. Sometimes it takes a while to reach those gates, and we may have to climb a tall mountain to walk through them, but they are always open.

As I thought about this wisdom practice, I reread a beautiful book by Thich Nhat Hanh called *Peace Is Every Step: The Path of Mindfulness in Everyday Life*. That idea captures what it means to live this wisdom practice. Every choice we make and step we take can be directed toward bringing about peace. The precise details of the steps are not always easy to discern. Taking them is a process of continual learning and experience. But it depends as much on what is inside of us as on what is outside. *Shalom* is wholeness, integrity, and a right relationship with ourselves. And when we let go and look forward, we move closer to it.

Forgiveness Clarifies

As we have seen, forgiveness is about much more than saying, "I forgive you." That oversimplification minimizes the hard work forgiveness requires. Forgiveness is one of our hardest wisdom practices. Expressing gratitude, performing acts of kindness, studying, and so forth are challenging, but they lack the emotional complexity and layers of self-exploration required by seeking and granting forgiveness. Part of the difficulty is the way forgiveness has been understood in our culture. We tend to think of forgiveness solely as a matter between two parties. The ex-boyfriend needed forgiveness from the woman he'd battered. She needed to grant forgiveness so he could have a clear conscience. Neither is true. *Forgiveness does not depend on the other party. It rests with us.*

That's part of why forgiveness—seeking and giving it— can contribute significantly to our well-being. It pushes us to change. It also pushes us to come to terms with what happened in the past. It encourages self-understanding. In so doing, it deepens our relationships. Because we can forgive, we can stay in relationships even when we make mistakes.

Forgiveness also lets us move on. It makes us stronger and more complete by acknowledging the broken parts of our lives. It reminds us that we can always grow and change. Forgiveness is the seedbed for new life.

Why We Need Faith to Forgive

The challenge, however, is that nothing in the natural world requires us to forgive. As we noted earlier, our default instinct when others hurt us is to want revenge. Forgiveness comes from seeing an inherent dignity in all people, and from modeling ourselves on a God Who forgives. This understanding helps us see why people of faith are often the quickest to forgive others and themselves. This willingness does not reflect the media caricature of people of religion as soft and naive. It reflects a belief that the ultimate path to happiness and well-being includes forgiveness.

In teaching about the connection between faith and forgiveness today, I have often turned to an extraordinary story told by best-selling author and journalist Malcolm Gladwell. Gladwell was raised as a Mennonite, and he tells of interviewing a Mennonite couple in his native Ontario. Their daughter was kidnapped and sexually molested. The police conducted the city's largest manhunt, and after several weeks they uncovered her body. She was frozen, her hands and feet bound.

After the funeral the father said, "We would like to know who the person or persons are who did this so we could share, hopefully, a love that seems to be missing in these people's lives." The mother added, "I can't say at this point I forgive this person," stressing the phrase *at this point*. "We have all done something dreadful in our lives, or have felt the urge to." The mother ultimately did forgive.

When he heard her words, Gladwell realized that *faith gives ordinary people extraordinary powers*. It does not relieve others of responsibility. The mother and father believed the full force of law should fall upon on the person who had murdered their daughter. Yet in the realm of interpersonal relationships, faith sometimes pushes us to do the opposite of what our natural inclinations dictate, and in so doing saves our lives. "A woman who walks away from the promise of power finds the strength to forgive—and saves her friendships, her marriage, and her sanity," Gladwell writes. The grieving mother rejected the power of seeking vengeance. She rejected the power of devoting her life to anger at the man who had murdered her daughter. These were her rights. We could hardly blame her if she had pursued them. Yet she did the opposite of what we would expect.

Moving on is not easy. Yet, as a devout Mennonite, she was prepared to do so. She knew God wanted her to forgive because she had prayed the words and studied the stories of God's forgiveness her entire life. Forgiveness was a habit she had developed. That's what Gladwell found remarkable. That's what faith had given her. Faith gives us the will and ability to do extraordinary things. And by doing those things, we live happier lives.

Making Forgiveness a Daily Practice

Some acts of forgiveness, as we have seen, are immensely difficult. Each of us will likely face such challenges in life. One of the ways we can prepare for them is by making forgiveness a habit. We can look for "peace in every step." It starts with accepting that we are not perfect. We make mistakes.

We see this idea in the Hebrew word for sin. It is *chet. Chet* is a term taken from archery, and it means "missing the mark."

A *chet* happens when we fail to do something we know is right, or we fail to resist doing something we know is wrong. We miss the mark.

What happens when we miss the mark? We grow distant from ourselves and others. In other words, a *chet* moves us away from another person and from God. If we are unnecessarily harsh with a sibling, for example, our acts create a distance between the two of us. Seeking forgiveness is a way of restoring the original closeness.

Jewish tradition offers a threefold path for achieving forgiveness when it comes to a *chet*: *regret, resolve, restore. Regret* is recognizing our mistake. It means we acknowledge what we did was wrong. We fail to feel regret if we simply recognize we caused harm to another person. That focuses the problem on them, not us. That's like saying we are sorry for how something we said *made the other person feel.* That's putting the responsibility on the other person, not ourselves. When we feel regret, we know we did something wrong.

Resolve is deciding on a way to express our regret. It means deciding not to bury our regret or avoid the discomfort of asking for forgiveness. After resolve comes *restore*. This part usually involves asking the wronged party for forgiveness. It also includes restitution. If we took something without asking, we need to return it. If we embarrassed someone in front of another person, we need to do something publicly to help restore their reputation. Sometimes the path to restitution is not clear cut. We need to be creative and thoughtful in looking for ways to make amends.

From a Jewish perspective, forgiveness involves both justice and grace. Justice comes from the way we assume responsibility and try our best to make restitution for our acts. Grace comes from the willingness of the other party (and God) to show empathy for our actions and accept our sincere efforts at restitution.

One of the ways we develop forgiveness as a habit is through visualization. Rabbi Zalman Shachter-Shalomi said we should take a moment every year and picture everyone who has hurt us sitting around our dinner table. We all share a meal and conversation. We talk and laugh. That's it. It's simple.

But what makes this visualization effective is that it is hard to be angry at guests we welcome into our home for a meal. This visualization doesn't work miracles, but it can pry our hearts open for a few minutes, and help us imagine what it might be like to be in restored relationship with someone who once wronged us. Picture that person and give it a try.

Look Inside and Commit
תלמוד תורה כנגד כלם

"The special quality of the road is to bring together God with its wayfarers.... Some walk the road for the sake of intimacy."
—Moses ben Jacob Cordovero (the RaMaK)

Three years ago, I realized that the Eilu Devarim prayer was speaking deeply to my condition. I discovered that this ancient prayer was a wisdom path around which I could shape my life. Since that day I've been trying to do just that, and I've been doing it with greater and lesser success. Some months it seems easy and pleasurable and inviting to live, with some intention, the practices offered by the prayer. Other months I get caught up in the hectic hustle and bustle of job, parenting, and marriage, and my focus seems to slip away.

So where I am on my own path, in my own life inside these ten practices, is in a space of discernment. I am discerning how best to live with the practices of my now most beloved prayer. And I am realizing that I might live with those practices very differently next year, or ten years from now. I am also realizing that an ongoing embrace of this prayer comes down to two things: discernment and commitment.

These two words are key to the last verse of our prayer because both words are translations of the Hebrew word *torah*. In Hebrew the final verse says *Talmud torah k'neged kulam*. We can interpret it as meaning, "Ongoing discernment of what is inside us and attention to our commitments give life meaning." In other words, if you seek meaning and happiness, look inside and commit to your path.

Setting Out on Your Path: Discernment

Last year my friend Ben joined a gym for the first time. He'd just turned forty, and he was seriously reevaluating many of his life habits, from how much time he spent at work to his relative lack of exercise. For the first three months of his new gym membership he was on fire for the gym. He practically lived there! He hired a trainer, whom he met three times a week. He tried out a spin class and a martial arts class and Krav Maga (Israeli self-defense techniques). He scheduled some sessions in the pool with a swim coach. He got into yoga and aquatic aerobics.

There was much my friend loved about his new gym-going. He loved the feeling that he was learning something new—and he understood, on a deep level, that even five years before he'd not had the inner courage to try something new, something he wasn't naturally good at. Ben also loved what he was learning by listening to his body. During the first few weeks, when his yoga teacher asked, "Where in your body do you feel the stretch?" Ben genuinely had no idea. By week four he'd begun to be able to answer that question. He also loved the easy camaraderie he was finding with other gym regulars; he'd expected them to be competitive, and he'd expected to feel intimidated by people who were more fit than he was, but although almost everyone *was* more fit than he was, he simply felt welcome.

And yet, after about four months, my friend realized he could not possibly keep up this new gym routine. In part that's because there's only so much time in the day, and Ben had begun letting other commitments slip in order to make time for the gym: he missed reading the morning newspaper in a leisurely way, and he regretted that his evening dog walk was now crimped because he got home ninety minutes later than he had before his gym obsession began. But perhaps more importantly, Ben realized he couldn't keep all his gym endeavors going because, simply, he didn't like some of them—he felt he *should* be learning to lift weights with a trainer, but he found that he had to force himself to go to his weight-lifting sessions, and try as he might to be present with his body during the weight lifting, he found himself thinking ahead to what he had to do the next day at work.

I thought of Ben recently when reading a book about spiritual practices in antiquity. In this book I learned that the word *asceticism* comes from the Greek term *askesis*, which can be translated as "exercise." The book I was reading went on to explain that the spiritual practices and spiritual disciplines we might adopt in the twenty-first century—from prayer to study to fasting to labyrinth walking—are forms of *askesis*; they are exercises. The author suggested parallels between spiritual exercises and physical, athletic exercises: they both take dedication, they both require a routine or a set of habits, and they both eventually leave us in excellent shape, so that if we ever need to sprint (physically or spiritually), we can.

All of those parallels between athletic exercises and spiritual exercises seem right to me, but in thinking about Ben I want to add another important parallel: Ben needed to discern which exercises were really right for him, which suited him—which exercises, you might say, he was really called to. And that is true of spiritual practice as well. Living the happiness prayer requires our discernment.

Each of our wisdom practices is good—yet no one person can do them all every day. We can't dedicate our mornings to kindness, our afternoons to Torah study, and our evenings to prayer. We can't properly mourn every death in the world and celebrate with every married couple. We need to focus. We need to discern.

And discernment is ongoing. We may begin something and then discern it does not fit who we are. After all, one has to be engaged in something before one can make any discernments, and no discernment is ever final—discerning what practices we are called to is a recurring task because sometimes our calling changes. Ben couldn't discern which athletic offerings he was really called to until he had been engaged in exercise for a while—and the exercise classes that suit him at forty might not be the same classes that suit him at forty-five.

When I first realized that the Eilu Devarim prayer was beckoning to me as a life path and as a collection of wisdom practices that would lead me back to deeper happiness and meaning, I was a little bit like Ben at the gym. I tried to throw myself into comforting mourners, visiting the sick, learning new things, praying, and forgiving. I even tried to write my parents a note every week, telling them something I appreciated about them. On the one hand, it wasn't so hard for me to do all these things—as a rabbi, I had a lot of them built into my job. But it was hard for me to do them all with *intention*. It was hard to do them all as *practices*. It was hard for me to receive them all *attentively*, as gifts that would lead me to happiness.

And so I began to notice, to discern. Ben's discernment began when he noticed that he didn't want to go to those weight-training sessions, and that he was thinking about his law firm while he was on the hip adductor machine. Similarly, I noticed that I was pretty distracted during morning prayer and that I was twitchy when trying to learn a new page of the Talmud (Jewish legal codes) every week. Ben decided to drop the weight training in order to have maximal—and maximally attentive—space for his spin class and his yoga class, ones he looked forward to and during which he felt, frankly, happy. Similarly, I decided that I didn't have to make myself pray every morning, and while I did need to study and learn new sacred texts, it was OK for me to spend some weeks learning other things, or simply reading for pleasure. Once I did that—once I eased up on the expectations I had of myself—I actually found I was more present in what I was already doing. I also felt I had more time and more focus for the pieces of the Eilu Devarim that were calling most to me—compelling me to visit people in the hospital and connect in a kind and honoring way with my parents.

It seems probable to me that over the course of a whole life, those callings will change. In this season of life, I am deeply drawn to study and kindness, but I am reasonably confident that in five years or ten years I'll be drawn to prayer and hospitality. In other words, the road back to happiness doesn't lead to a fixed terminus. There's always another bend in the road, and around that bend we discover a new invitation to happiness—and, in fact, leave an old invitation behind. That's why discernment is ongoing. The practices that you find most nourishing right now may not be the practices you most need next year.

How to Discern What You Need

Discernment is a formal, spiritual-sounding word, but it's pretty simple to practice on the ground. It almost always starts with noticing. In fact, *noticing* is a pretty good synonym for discernment. You can begin right now. Which chapters of this book were you most engaged in, and which were you most bored by? Which chapters did you underline and asterisk, and which did you skip?

One tip: *engagement* doesn't necessarily mean "attraction." Your deepest engagement with a chapter might have been to argue with the chapter. The chapter might have made you feel unexpectedly angry or sad. A calling, in other words, can come in many different emotional shapes. One of our wisdom practices might have seemed very attractive to you; the chapter on comforting mourners or on learning might have left you feeling energized and inspired; it might have fired up your imagination. If so, the energy and inspiration and imagining could very well be a call—a hint from your truest self that this is a practice you want to take up.

But similarly, you might have felt unsettled, or unnerved, by a chapter. Those emotions are equally worth paying attention to. Sometimes a call comes in the form of agitation or irritation, as the irritant of a grain of sand causes an oyster to produce a pearl.

If you were agitated or saddened or angered by one of the practices or by one of the chapters, that might be because you have some inner work to do around a given theme. Pursuing a practice that makes you feel uplifted and energized will surely lead you into happiness, but pursuing a practice that irritates or saddens you ultimately might too, because that pursuit can help you get to the bottom of whatever provokes you.

So which chapters called to you with inspiration and energy or with a more complex, unnerving emotion? Answer that question and begin your deeper journey.

Setting Out on Your Path: Commitment

Once you have discerned—once you have noticed which practice or practices are beckoning to you—the next step is to commit to a practice. Wisdom practices, spiritual practices, require a special kind of commitment: *experimental, flexible, generous* commitment.

By "experimental commitment" I mean a playful and curious commitment by which you are seeking to discover how the practice in question can best fit into your life. Let's say that the practice that most clearly called to you was the practice of learning. After hearing the call to learning, you probably need to experiment with different ways your life can actually accommodate it. Some people might make a radical change—going back to school for the college degree they always wanted, or undertaking a time-intensive apprenticeship in the art of massage therapy or cooking. Other people might sign up for tennis lessons. Still other people might decide simply to be more attentive to what they might learn when they are helping their tweens with math homework. And yet others might determine that they want to read more. But what will they read? Well, that might require some experimenting.

Maybe you decide you are going to finally "read the classics," or reread everything you were assigned in high school English classes now that you are finally old enough to appreciate them! But as you are plowing through *The Grapes of Wrath*, you might realize that you'd like someone to process the reading with—and so you change your experiment a bit, and instead of engaging in solitary classics reading, you join a neighborhood book club. The basic commitment to engage in *learning* is there, but you're experimenting with different modes of learning, trying to see what suits you best.

By "flexible commitment," I mean that just as different wisdom practices may call to you at different life stages, the ways you engage a given practice might change too. My friend Lauren has always been interested in prayer—since she was a young girl, it has been a part of her life. But the particular kinds of praying she's been drawn to have changed. During some seasons she has prayed almost entirely from prayer books. During other seasons she has prayed primarily through doodling! And during yet other seasons she has been drawn to breath prayer. In all these seasons, she has remained engaged with the practice of prayer, but she's been flexible about the exact shape her prayers take.

Finally, "generous commitment." By this I mean cutting yourself a little slack—not so much slack that the commitment evaporates, but enough that you can remain engaged with the practice you've chosen (or, maybe, the practice that has chosen you). Most of us have had the experience of making a New Year's resolution—to slash refined sugar consumption, or to run every day, or to bite our tongue when we feel an impulse to be sharp with our spouse or kids. We're really good at sticking to this resolution for two or three weeks, and then at the first slip—the first slice of cake or missed jog—we give up.

"Well, I've already failed," we might think. "Obviously I am not cut out for jogging." And then we quit. Generous commitment involves being generous with ourselves. When we are committed with generosity, we are able to say, "I didn't jog today, but I am not a failure. I'll plan to go on a shorter jog tomorrow," or "I didn't jog today, but I am not a failure.

Tomorrow I'll take an extra half hour to drive to my favorite out-of-the-way park and treat myself by running in a landscape I really love." Similarly, you might not manage to get your book club novel read one month—that's OK! A person of generous commitment goes to the book club meeting anyway and says, "I have not read the book, but I wanted to learn from others' responses to it." (And in doing so, you also give the other book club members an opportunity to forgive!)

Experimental, flexible, generous commitment always comes back to discernment, to noticing. In a life of experimental, flexible, generous commitment, there are always opportunities to discern—for example, to discern why, in year four of the book club, you're more and more often not reading the book. Maybe in that noticing is another call, to move away from the book club and take up a different kind of learning. Or maybe in that noticing is a call away from learning and toward a wholly different wisdom practice—you've been skipping book club because you've been making chicken soup for the bereaved in your community; your own choices are telling you, perhaps, that you're being called away from study and into the work of comforting the mourner. Or perhaps you're being called to redouble your engagement with study, to press through the boredom and distraction and find a *deeper* happiness. So knowing how to live inside your commitment requires discernment.

Discernment and commitment have been my constant companions as I live the happiness prayer.

The Road Back to Happiness

I opened this chapter with two teachings from a sixteenth-century Jewish mystic known as the Ramak. The Ramak followed other Jewish thinkers in recognizing that the road can be a place of danger and that because it is a place of danger, God is especially felt by travelers on a road. The Ramak and other Jewish teachers were thinking of literal, physical roads, which do indeed hold all sorts of dangers in store for travelers. But their insight also applies to the metaphorical road of spiritual practices. The danger of spiritual practice is not that you might get hit by a car or robbed by a stranger. It is that *you will change*—and even good changes, even changes in the direction of happiness and meaning, can seem, at times, dangerous. God is especially, even protectively, present to people who embark on such a road. God is with us as we change and grow. God will be with you as you change through the happiness prayer.

A second teaching the RaMaK provides about roads has to do with the purpose of walking on a road. You shouldn't walk on a road for a worldly purpose, wrote the RaMaK—not to become more successful or to win friends and influence people. Rather, you should walk on the road "for the sake of intimacy." For intimacy with all that is holy. For intimacy with your true self. For intimacy with what really makes you happy.

In fact, it might be a little misleading to say that this prayer, our ten wisdom practices, is a road back to happiness, because that makes it sound as if happiness is a far-off destination at which we arrive once, after a really long trek.

Happiness actually isn't a onetime, far-off destination. Happiness is the path, and we find it through the journey.

Will We Ever Be Happy?

I started this journey with the happiness prayer just as my second child was born. She is now eight, and my oldest is ten. I've begun to see their character develop. I've begun to think about their futures. And my wife and I have also seen them experience some of life's ups and downs. They are becoming aware of what they are and are not good at. They are experiencing the ways friendships can come and go. They have become aware of death and loss.

Like most parents, I want my children to be happy. I'd like to protect them from the inevitable pains and struggles they will face. But in living the happiness prayer, I've learned that true happiness does not come from ease. It does not come from getting whatever we want whenever we want. It comes from meaning. It comes from doing things that make a difference. It comes from knowing we are here for a reason.

The happiness prayer is a lifeline for reminding us of these truths. When we experience the ups and downs of life, we have a path to which we can return. We have a compass pointing us back to the right road. It is a road where we honor the past, walk with kindness, and learn continuously. It is a road where we celebrate good times, invite people into our lives, and are there for others in pain and in grief. It is a road where we stop and pray, where we forgive, and where we commit to living with intention and discernment.

I know that if I continue to walk that road, my congregation and my children are more likely to follow and end up a little happier. And if you commit to it and bring the happiness prayer into your life, so will you.

Happiness Quick Start Guide

Here are five questions for each of the ten chapters on practices that result in well-being. These questions will help you begin to live by the happiness prayer. I chose them carefully, using both contemporary research on the study of happiness and what I have seen work in classes and seminars I have led. You can ask these questions of yourself. Or you can discuss them with a partner or in a group setting. If you discuss them and write down your answers, you can send them to me at evan@rabbi .me, and I will offer feedback. Shalom.

Honor Those Who Gave You Life

1. What is the difference between honoring your father and mother and loving them?
2. If you were one of Mary's children, how would you have responded to the news of her death?
3. Think about the evolution of your relationship with your parents. How did you honor them when you were in your twenties? What about your teens? How do you honor them today?
4. Must parents honor their children?
5. Did Viktor Frankl make the right choice in deciding to stay in Austria?

Be Kind

1. *Chesed* is a Hebrew word referring to kindness within our relationships. In what relationships is kindness most important?
2. Who comes to mind when you think of kindness? What did they do and what did they say?
3. Have you ever wanted to act with kindness toward someone but felt yourself stopped by something? What was it? How would you act differently if you could redo that scene?
4. Does suffering lead to kindness? Does having experienced a certain kind of pain make us more empathetic to others experiencing it?
5. Think about a time when someone bought something for you. Now think about a time when you bought something for someone else. Which experience made you happier?

Keep Learning

1. What are your memories of school? Did learning make you happy, or was it more an ordeal you had to endure?
2. If you could take a sabbatical and learn about anything you wished for six months, what would you choose?
3. What passion from your childhood do you most wish to reclaim? What steps would it take for you to do so?
4. What lessons have you learned from your work? From your family? From your community?
5. What lessons do you wish to pass to your children or grandchildren or those you mentor? What lessons do you wish to pass on to the next generation?

Invite Others into Your Life

1. Who has made you feel most welcome in their life and their home? What other qualities did that person display?
2. Do you open up your home to others? What stops you from doing so more often?
3. What experience in another person's home most surprised you or changed your life?
4. Why do we tend to bring gifts when we are guests in another's home?
5. What does the word *hospitality* mean to you?

Be There When Others Need You

1. Who called or visited you the last time you were sick? What else about that person stands out to you?
2. Do you pray when you are sick? How does it feel?
3. What are the most comforting words someone has said to you during a difficult time?
4. Has prayer ever made you feel uncomfortable?
5. Have you ever witnessed what seemed like a miraculous healing? What happened?

Celebrate Good Times

1. Do you feel happier when you are around happy people?
2. What biblical verse makes you feel happiest? If you can't come up with a biblical verse, think of a quote from another source.
3. What are the liminal moments of your life, your key times of transition or turning points? Try to recall how you felt before and after them.

4. What person or experience in your life has given you the greatest joy? Can you pinpoint what gave you that joy?

5. What is the most memorable communal experience of your life? It could be a wedding, a birthday party, or something similar.

Support Yourself and Others during Times of Loss

1. Do you believe a funeral or memorial service can ever be called a celebration of life? Why or why not?

2. If you have experienced a significant loss, what brought the greatest comfort in the days and weeks immediately following?

3. Do you know anyone who has never been able to recover from a loss? What has stopped them?

4. Has writing your thoughts or feelings ever helped you through a difficult time?

5. Do you have eight to ten people in your life you could call at two a.m.? If not, what do you need to do to find them?

Pray with Intention

1. At what moments has prayer been most powerful and meaningful for you?

2. Do you believe God answers our prayers? How does God do so?

3. Do you pray words from a page or words from your heart?

4. Which prayers speak most to you? Why?

5. How does prayer change one's character?

Forgive

1. Have you ever refused to forgive someone? Do you regret not doing so?

2. What prevents us from offering forgiveness without reservation or hesitation?

3. Is forgiving the same as condoning?

4. Think of a person who has forgiven you. How did it change your relationship?

5. Is love never having to say you're sorry? Or is love having to say you're sorry every fifteen minutes?

Look Inside and Commit

1. What projects have you started but not finished?

2. What qualities do you notice in happy people? How can you cultivate them?

3. What habits do you have today that you did not have five years ago?

4. Is there a person or a project you need to commit yourself to over the next ninety days?

5. What one change will make you happier in the year ahead?

Acknowledgments

This is my first book with Hachette/Center Street, and I am grateful to its team for their support and trust. Special thanks to my editors Adrienne Ingrum, Andrea Glickson, Grace Tweedy, and their entire team. My agent, Carol Mann, brought me to Hachette, and she is truly a writer's agent, helping with ideas and drawing from her experience and wisdom to find me the right home. I am also grateful to Lauren F. Winner, who provided an extraordinary reading of the text and great insights for making it more succinct and meaningful.

My wife, Rabbi Ari Moffic, helps me sharpen every idea and does not hesitate to tell me when something I think is brilliant really doesn't measure up. Aside from that, she is the most wonderful partner, the greatest source of happiness in my life, and mom to our kids, Hannah and Allie. I am grateful to all of them for not complaining too much when I constantly opened up my computer during vacations to read through drafts and make a few more edits.

My parents, Rusti and Steve Moffic, are both wonderful writers and role models, and their insight and love helped me every step of the way. Thanks as well to my sister, Stacia, and her family for reminding me how essential family is to true happiness and meaning.

Pastor David Wood helped find the right title and has

become a wonderful friend. Melissa Mondschain read an early draft of the text and gave me valuable feedback. I am also grateful to all the churches and synagogues who have invited me to speak and inspired me to write this book, including David Lyon, John Linder, Joann Forest, Roberta Ingersoll, Chris Chakoian, Aaron Niequist, Wes Avram, Jerry Bolyn, Tom Hurley, and so many others.

This book is dedicated to the members of Congregation Solel, the spiritual home I am blessed to serve as rabbi. Their trust and encouragement give me the opportunity to live, serve, and love in a way that brings meaning and happiness to my life.

Index

About the Author

Evan Moffic helps people of all faiths use ancient Jewish wisdom to find more meaning and joy in daily life. He writes regularly for the Huffington Post and Beliefnet. He has spoken at Jewish book festivals and more than one hundred synagogues, churches, and organizational gatherings and appeared as a news commentator on social and religious issues. He was an esteemed guest at the president's annual White House Chanukah Party in 2014 and 2015.

He is also the author of three books: *What Every Christian Needs to Know about the Jewishness of Jesus*, which was featured in the *Washington Post*, the *Chicago Tribune*, *Publishers Weekly*, and dozens of other publications and podcasts; *What Every Christian Needs to Know about Passover*, which was the focus of a lead story for *Christianity Today*; and most recently *Shalom for the Heart*, which uses short devotionals to draw from biblical teachings in the search for peace of mind.

At age thirty he became the youngest senior rabbi of a large congregation in the United States. His congregation became the fastest-growing synagogue in metropolitan Chicago. Rabbi Moffic continues to lead Congregation Solel in suburban Chicago, and he and his wife, Rabbi Arielle Moffic, have married and counseled more than five hundred interfaith couples, working with them on an ongoing basis to help them bring Jewish wisdom and practices into their families. They are the parents of Hannah (2007) and Allie (2009).

A graduate of Stanford University, Rabbi Moffic was ordained as a rabbi by the Reform movement's Hebrew Union College-Jewish Institute of Religion in 2006. As the child of a psychiatrist, Rabbi Moffic has always been interested in the connection between psychology and spirituality. He and his father, Dr. H. Steven Moffic, have presented together at the American Psychiatric Association.